The Nature of CAPITALISM!

(A List of the EVILS of CAPITALISM!)

By
The Worldwide People's Revolution!®

Book 038 ★ ♥

(The Cover shows a Photograph of a Pretty Red Car. P-5989)

Copyright, Dedication and Introduction

By our Selected King's Chief Editor — Doctor Samuel Walker Edison, Ph.D., MA., BS and QC!

ISBN — 13: 978-1727-7688-86
ISBN — 10: 1727-7688-84

00-01 [_] This Exceptionally Good Book is COPYRIGHTED AD 2018, by the Selected King of **The Worldwide People's Revolution!®**, who is the Inspired Author of more than 350 Good Books, including the New MAGNIFIED Version (NMV) of the entire *Bible, the Book of Mormon, the Book of Ahikar, the Koran,* and a Multitude of Original Books of his own: beCause he is "The King of the Birds," you might say, or the King of the Great Philosophers, as the Greeks would say, who are Symbolized by PEACOCKS, whose Tales of Truths spring out of them Naturally: beCause God has Blest them with a Special Gift, which becomes Obvious after reading a few pages of their Extremely Good Books — such as: **"The New MAGNIFIED Version of the Book of ACTS!" (The Understandable Version of the ACTS of the Apostles in Plain English!)**, Book 063, or: **"Justifications for Capitalizations!" (WHY our Elected King Defies the School of FOOLS by Capitalizing LOVE and HATE!) By The Worldwide People's Revolution!®**

00-02 [_] All Rights are Reserved for Honest Capitalists with Right Minds, who are still Able to THINK and Remember, who will Confess that Capitalism has some Great Weaknesses: beCause it is *"the Love of Money"* in ACTION, which is the Root Cause for almost all Evils, including "Terrorism," Poverty, Hunger, Riots, Strikes, Police Brutalities, Election Deceptions, and Civil Wars! Yes, Capitalism is Directly or Indirectly Linked with almost all Evils within this World of Woes, even as our Selected King has Proven within his Good Books, which no one on this Earth has Proven to be WRong by any Means. {See www.Amazon.com for: **"The Root Cause for almost all Evils!" (The Strange Things that People Say and Do to Get more Money!) By The Worldwide People's Revolution!®** Book 078, which is a Companion Book of: **"For the Love of Money!"** Book 003.}

00-03 [_] No Portion of this Inspired Book shall be Reproduced by any Means for Sale without Written Permission from the Publishers. However, with that Permission, anyone in the World may make Perfect Copies of this Book, or of any other Books by **The Worldwide People's Revolution!®**, and Sell them for a Fair Profit, and KEEP 90 percent of the Net Profits for their own Prosperity: beCause our Selected King only wants 10% of the Net Profits for the Construction of **"The Great World TEMPLE of PEACE,"** which will be the Headquarters for **"The New RIGHTEOUS One-World Government,"** which will be the Tallest and Largest Building in the World, being nearly a Mile Tall and 8+ Miles in Diameter, having 60 Great Terraces with 6 Smaller Terraces within each Great Terrace, having tens of thousands of Beautiful Stone Dome Home Complexes built into the Terraces, which will be Planted with Fruit and Nut Trees, Grape Vines, Vegetable and Flower Gardens: beCause all of the Elected Officials of the New Righteous One-World Government will Live and Work within that Great Temple, along with their thousands of Voluntary Servants, who will be Contented with Foods, Drinks and Clothing.

(A List of the EVILS of CAPITALISM!)

00-04 [_] This Special Book is now DEDICATED to the Deceived Masses of People in this World of Woes, who have been Sold a Capitalist Pack of Outlandish LIES, who Actually Believe that there is no Better Way to Live than the American Way, most of whom are now Living in Wooden / Plastic Firetrap Mouse-infested Cockroach Dens, which can Burn Up in less than one Hour, Blow Away in a Tornado in less than one Minute, get Eaten Up by Termites, have their Roofs Beaten to Death by Hailstones, be Buried under Mudslides, be Shaken Down in Earthquakes, be Covered Up by Volcanoes, be Flooded by Hurricanes or Overflowing Rivers, or otherwise be Destroyed by one Means or another: beCause they are Designed by the Members of the Synagogue of SATAN, to put it in Biblical Terms, who is the Chief Capitalist! Yes, he is the Father of all LIES, including that Lie about Capitalism being "the Economic Salvation of Mankind," when it is Actually what has Caused most of Mankind's Massive Problems — such as Mountains Trash and Unbearable Pollution in Industrialized Nations like China, where a Person can hardly Breathe: beCause of the LUST for more Money, which has Produced Drug Pushers, for Example, who have Sold TRILLIONS of Dollars-worth of DRUGS, which is the Chief Capitalist Business in the World! Yes, the Drug Addicts have been Sold a BIG FAT LIE — that one cannot be Healthy nor Happy without the Use of DRUGS, which the American Bisons are Laughing at: beCause they have Lived for Millions of Years without any Drugs at all, along with Monkeys and Apes in Africa! ‡ {See: **"Did God or Satan Ordain Medical Doctors?" (Ask Huck Finn and/or Nigger Jim: because neither Tom Sawyer nor Judge Thatcher would Know!) By The Worldwide People's Revolution!®**, Book 022, which is a Companion Book of: **"The LUSCIOUS All-Mineral Organic Method of Gardening!" (HOW to Grow DELICIOUS Satisfying Foods for Potential Kingz and Kweenz in Beautiful Swanky PALACES!)**, Book 021, which is a Companion Book of: **"Orgimmick Gardening at its Best!" (HOW to Grow Delicious Satisfying Foods without a 10-Million-Dollar Investment!) By The Worldwide People's Revolution!®**, Book 079, which contains many Colored Photographs with Explanations! See also: **"Beautiful Swanky PALACES!" (A New Concept in Living Habits — Swanky Palaces for Poor People!) By The Worldwide People's Revolution!®** Book 066.}

00-05 [_] O Doctor Samuel Walker Edison, are you not Educated enough to Know about the GOODNESS of Drugs? Are you not Aware that all Wild Animals have been Using Drugs ever since Adam and Eve were Cast Out of the Garden of Good Eating? Well, let me tell you something, which is Educational — GOD, himself, is the Chief Druggist, who Created all of those Drugs, including Modern Chemical Drugs like METH and LSD. Therefore, do not Speak Evil of our GOOD Drugs, much less the Bad Foods and Good Drugs Administration (FDA). †§‡§§

00-06 [_] Well, I Challenge you to Find so much as ONE Wild Animal on the Earth, who has ever Consumed any Kind of Drugs: beCause it is Unnatural, Unnecessary, and Universally INSANE! In Fact, Trillions of Animals Lived Well for thousands and perhaps for Millions of Years without the Use of any Drugs, even as the American Bisons roamed on the Great Plains for thousands of Years without the Assistance of any Doctor Drug Pushers, and none of them were Screaming with PAINS — even as our Selected King has been Living without those Pains and Drugs for more than 50 Years! Indeed, Jesus Christ said, *"You shall Learn the Truth, and the Whole Truth will Set you Free in all Ways when you Practice it."* — The Gospel According to Saint Bartholomew.

00-07 [_] O Doctor Sam, there is no Gospel of Saint Bartholomew in my *Hole Bible;* and therefore, I do not Believe that such a Statement is True, even if it can be Proven in a Courtroom, at: **"The GREAT Worldwide TELEVISED Court HEARING!" (That Great Meeting of the Most**

(A List of the EVILS of CAPITALISM!)

Intelligent and Well-Educated Minds!) By The Worldwide People's Revolution!® Book 041: beCause I am a General Bonehead Sloth-gut Windbag Hole-in-my-Head, who Suffers with Chronic Constipation of the Mind! After all, if our Modern Medical Establishment is not the Chief Servant of Almighty God, I am going to Stop Attending the Unholy Church of Graceful Sinners on Suicide Avenue and Mockingbird Lane, which Teaches the Whole Truth and nothing but the Whole Truth: beCause they Believe every Word that Proceeded out of the Mouths of the GODS, one of whom was Jesus Christ, himself, who was Praying in the Garden of Gethsemane to his Father God, saying: *"Father, not my Will be Done on this Earth; but, may your Will be Done on the Earth, even as it is now Done in Heavenly Places, where they have more than 10 Million Varieties of Drugs to Choose from for Curing their Ailments — Thanks to your Everlasting Mercies, who Created Mosquitoes, Ticks, Fleas, Lice, Mice, Rats, Bedbugs, Weevils, Fire Ants, Hornets, Snakes, Scorpions, Germs, Worms, Bacterias, and all Kinds of PESTS to Torment Humanity, and to Kill no less than a Million Children with Malaria, every Year: because of your Love for them! Halleluiah! Moreover, beCause of thy Great Love for Mankind, you have Inspired Inventive Men to make all Kinds of Labor-saving Tools — such as Automobiles for Transportation, whereby Mankind can be Saved from Walking, and thus get so Obese as to not be Able to Walk! Praise the LORD, O God! And as for my Sufferings on the Torture Stake, I will Gladly do it for the Sakes of those Rich Edomite Bankers, who Live in Swanky Palaces, who have Collected 90 percent of the Wealth in this World of Wonders for their own Sensual Pleasures, whom I Envy: because I have not even had a Pillow to lay my Head on at Night, being just a little Lower than a Hobo along the Railroad; or a Beggar, who Lives in the Sewage Drains under the Streets. Nevertheless, I Thank thee, O Father God, that I do not Suffer with Chronic Constipation of the Mind, like those Scribes and Pharisees, who Judge me to be nothing but an Ignorant Fool, in spite of being Able to Walk on the Water, Transform Water into Wine, and Raise Up Extinct Creatures, whereby the Natural Balance of Life on the Earth might be Restored to its Original Condition, which had no Mosquitoes, Ticks, Bedbugs, Weevils, Scorpions, nor Fleas, which were brought into this World by Aliens from other Worlds by Satan and Sons, Incorporated, whereby they might have Excuses for Inventing and Selling Various Kinds of those Wonderful Drugs, and thus Fill their Pockets and Bank Accounts with Money — Thanks to Capitalism, which is the Economic System of Satan! Amen."* — *The Edomite Banker's Version in Plain English.* §§ {See: **"Are we Tax Slaves of a Lower Order than those Lying EDOMITES!"** (HOW to be Liberated from all Slavery, Worldwide!) By The Worldwide People's Revolution!®, Book 052, plus another Wonderful Books, called: **"SWANGKEENOMIKS Rules the Roost!"** (HOW all People can Prosper in a RIIT WAA, and STOP Polluting the Earth with Capitalist TRASH!) By The Worldwide People's Revolution!® Book 039.}

00-08 [_] Well, in that Case, you will likely go on Suffering in your Miserable State of Extreme Poverty, while Vainly Imagining that you are Rich and Increased with Goods, and have Need for NOTHING, including the Inspired Words of Provable Truths that God has Revealed to our Selected King, who can Honestly say that he is FREE with a Capital F, while you are a Prisoner of a very Sick Society of Capitalist IDIOTS, who are otherwise known as: EDUCATION SLAVES, Work Slaves, TAX SLAVES, Insurance Slaves, INTEREST SLAVES, Drug Slaves, ELECTRICKERY BILLS SLAVES, Food Bills Slaves, TRANSPORTATION SLAVES, Gas Bills Slaves, WATER BILLS SLAVES, Rent Slaves, REPAIR BILLS SLAVES, Childcare Slaves, ENTERTAINMENT BILLS SLAVES, Telephone Bills Slaves, and ENDLESS BILLS SLAVES, who have no Idea HOW to Escape from that SLAVERY! Moreover, it is unlikely that you will Finish Reading this Inspired Book: beCause you Suffer with Chronic Constipation of the Mind, whereby Great Truths do not even make Good Sense to you, when they should be and would be Gems of Truths within the Golden Crown on your Holy Head, if you were a True SAINT. {See www.Amazon.com for: **"The Gospel According to our Elected King!" (The Good News from the Most Modern Perspective!) By The Worldwide People's Revolution!®**, Book 077, which is a Companion Book of: **"HOW to Become a HOLY Man!" (40 Good Reasons WHY People Should FAST and PRAY!)**, Book 045, which is a Companion Book of: **"The Proper RULES for FASTING!" (The Complete Instruction Manual for True Repentance!) By The Worldwide People's Revolution!®** Book 046.}

00-09 [_] So, O Doctor Samuel Walker Edison, if Capitalism is so BAD, why is it Accepted by so many Professing "Christians," Worldwide?

00-10 [_] Well, if you had been Raised in a Family of Hindus, in India, for Example, what would be your Chances of Learning anything about *the Book of Mormon?* Probably no Chance at all, in spite of the Fact that a Good Mormon is Equally as Good as a Good Hindu, and a Good Hindu is Equally as Good as a Good Muslim, and a Good Muslim is Equally as Good as a Good Christian, and a Good Christian is Equally as Good as a Good Buddhist, and a Good Buddhist is Equally as Good as a Good Mennonite, and so on: beCause Good People are GOOD, while Evil People are EVIL, no matter what their Religious and/or Political Beliefs might be: beCause their Goodness or Evilness is not Measured by their BELIEFS so much as by their ACTIONS, which Speak Louder than their Beliefs, which may only be Superficial, as in the Case of most Capitalist Christians, who have never even Thought about the List of the EVILS of Capitalism: beCause, like those Hindus, they have not been Taught anything about the Evils of Capitalism, even as the Hindus have not been Taught anything about **"The New MAGNIFIED Version of The Book of MORMON!" (The Story of the White and Dark Indians in the Americas!) By The Worldwide People's Revolution!®**, Book 040, much less Study it, which is Equally as Good, and maybe Better, than any Religious Book that they might be Studying! Yes, it is just a Case of IGNORANCE in all such Cases. Trust me, Capitalism has what Appears to be Good Aspects: beCause X-amount of People seem to Prosper by Means of Capitalism; but, are Automobiles, for Example, GOOD in the Eyes of GOD, who Judges According to Reality? Indeed, Cars can Rightly be Blamed for the Deaths of MILLIONS of People, even as Wars can Rightly be Blamed for the Gory Bloody Deaths of hundreds of Millions of People! Therefore, both Cars and Wars are Obviously BAD, even if no one Wants to Confess it, even as Drug Addictions, Gluttony, and Drunkenness are BAD. The Good News is this: our Selected King Explains how to Raise our Standard of Living by many Times without the Use of Capitalism, which is the Love of Money in Action, which is Different than Free Enterprise, which can be Good. Yes, he Explains how almost everyone can become Moderately RICH, without Telling any Lies, nor Selling any Trash, whereby even the Poorest People in the World can now get Moderately RICH, and without even going to College! Guaranteed! And now I ask you this very Important Question for you to Meditate on: "Would you BUY anything in this World, if it Costed thousands of Dollars, and had a hundred or more Disadvantages, and could even KILL you; or, would you not Prefer to Buy something with NO Disadvantages, which could Save your Life, and could NOT Kill you by any Means; but, that has more than 5,000 Advantages?" Please Check the Appropriate Box and/or Boxes below. {See: **"Beautiful Swanky PALACES!" (A New Concept in Living Habits — Swanky Palaces for Poor People!) By The Worldwide People's Revolution!®** Book 066.}

(A List of the EVILS of CAPITALISM!)

A-[_] I would NOT Buy anything that I Know could Kill me, or someone else, and especially if it were Expensive, and were Guaranteed to end up in the Trash: beCause I am NOT STUPID!

B-[_] I would have to Know what the Advantages and Disadvantages are for Buying it.

C-[_] I would Buy it, if my Mother or Father would Buy it: beCause I Trust them.

D-[_] I would not Buy it, if it were a BAD Thing in God's Opinion. But, who Knows for Sure what God's Opinion is about anything? Does God have an Opinion about Pollution?

E-[_] I would Buy it, if it might make my Life Easier, even if it Kills me. For Example, I Spray Cancer-causing Round-up on the Unwanted Grasses and Weeds: so that I do not have to Hoe Out those Grasses and Weeds in my Garden, which Saves me from a LOT of Difficult Work, whereby I can Save some of my FAT for the Long Cold Winter. †§‡§§

F-[_] If I could Live Well without it, and even have a Higher Standard of Living without it, I would not Buy it. For Example, rather than use Poisonous Round-up in the Garden, I would use Swanky Mulching Rocks, which have 50 Advantages for using them. Indeed, you can see Pictures of them with Explanations in: **"Orgimmick Gardening at its Best!" (HOW to Grow Delicious Satisfying Foods without a 10-Million-Dollar Investment!) By The Worldwide People's Revolution!® Book 079.** Amaze yourself!

G-[_] God Knows that I do not Want to Say nor Do any Evil Thing; but, HOW am I supposed to Judge what Things are Good and what Things are EVIL?

H-[_] I Believe that whatever Glorifies God is GOOD, and whatever Dishonors God is EVIL. And therefore, this is an EVIL Book: beCause it Dishonors the God of Creation, who Inspired Inventors to make all Kinds of Vehicles, which Pollute the Air, Water, Land, Plants, Animals, and Peoples with Harmful Chemical Abominations, which are likely the Chief Causes for Climate Changes, Radical Weather Patterns, and Insane Thinking. †§‡§§

I-[_] I Believe that there are some Things in this World that are both Good and Evil. For Example, Cars and Pickup Trucks are Good for Transporting People and their Things all about, which is GOOD; but, at the same Time, those Cars and Pickups can KILL us, if some Drunkard runs into us, or if the Brakes should Fail, which would be EVIL. †§‡§§

J-[_] I am Greatly Confused by the Facts. Nevertheless, I Believe that True Justice Demands that all Good Things have NO Evil Characteristics. For Example, Polished Marble does not Require any Painting to Look Good; but, Rusty Metals must be Painted to Look Good, and Prevent them from more Rusting. Therefore, Paints and Solvents are GOOD, and Children should Sniff on them to get High: because all of the Holy Angels do it, whom I have Seen in the Junkyards of America, Dancing with Insanity Clauses. †§‡§§

K-[_] King Jesus would not Use Toxic Paints, nor Harmful Solvents: beCause they Harm our Environment. Therefore, all such Toxic Paints and Solvents are no Good. However, Capitalism could not Function without them. †§‡

L-[_] Lots of Laughs! King Jesus would not even Ride in a Car: beCause it is Toxic to our Environment, and should therefore be against the Law to Produce it.

M-[_] If it is a Matter of Money, and Saving our Great False Economy, we should Buy it, even if it Kills us: beCause that is what Jesus would Do, and I am not Crazy. †§‡§§

N-[_] Not everyone is as Crazy as you are. Jesus would not Say nor Do anything to Protect the Great False Economy. To Hell with the Great False Economy. {See: **"The Great False Economy is now DEBUNKED!" (Adolf Hitler had a much Better Economic System!) By The Worldwide People's Revolution!® Book 053.**}

O-[_] Are there no Options? Can we not Use Cars Wisely, and not Pollute the Air, Water, nor Land with Toxic Poisons? Can we not Compromise our Moral Values to Do Business with the Devil in this World of Woes? {See: **"The Environmentalists' Paradise!" (HOW almost Everyone could be Living in a Beautiful Manmade Paradise!) By The Worldwide People's Revolution!®, Book 035**, which is a Companion Book of: **"Beautiful Swanky PALACES!" (A New Concept in Living Habits — Swanky Palaces for Poor People!) By The Worldwide People's Revolution!®, Book 066**, which is a Companion Book of: **"Guaranteed Solutions!" (HOW to Solve our Local and Global Problems in the Most Rational Manner Possible!) By The Worldwide People's Revolution!®, Book 080**, which is a Companion Book of: **"Are Americans the Most STUPID People who ever Lived?" (HOW Working People can PROSPER and Live in PEACE Under the Rulership of a RIGHTEOUS KING!) By The Worldwide People's Revolution!®, Book 047**, which is a Companion Book of: **"All of the Arguments are in Favor of our Selected King, who has Zero Challengers!" (Before you Attend another Election Deception, you should Carefully Study this Inspired Book with an Honest Open Mind!) By The Worldwide People's Revolution!® B-085.**}

P-[_] People should be Wise, and thus Love and Obey GOD: beCause he is the Final Judge and Great Rewarder. Therefore, if God is Against us for having Noisy Polluting Cars: beCause of the Multitude of Great Disadvantages for having them, then we are Cursed by them: beCause he said, *"You shall not bring any Abomination into your House, lest you become a Cursed Thing like it."* — See Deuteronomy 7. Moreover, *"To him who Knows to Do Good, and he does not Do it, to him it is a SIN."* — James 4:17, RNKJV. Therefore, if those **"GLORIOUS Swanky Hotels Castles and Fortresses!" (Beautiful Planned City States for WISE Intelligent Well-Educated People with Common Sense and Good Understanding!)**, Book 019, just Happen to have more than 5,000 Good Reasons and Great Advantages for Building them and Living within the Borders of them, we should Do GOOD by Building them and Living within them: beCause they have ZERO Great Disadvantages for Righteous People! Indeed, Criminals will NOT Like them: beCause they are Criminals; but, all Righteous People will LOVE them, and be Liberated from all Forms of Slavery, some of which are Listed in Verse 00-08. Selah. ‡ {See: **"The Seven Basic Spiritual Building Blocks of LIFE!" (Faith Hope Trust Love Patience Persistence and Obedience!) By The Worldwide People's Revolution!®, Book 036**, which is a Companion Book of: **"God Speaks and the Whole World Listens!" (Fire on the Mountain from the Burning Bush by the Spirit of Truth!) Book 026.**}

(A List of the EVILS of CAPITALISM!)

Q-[_] The Great Question is this: **"Will God Condemn us for Utilizing the Material Things that he has Blest us with, if we are Selfish with them, and do not Use them Wisely for everyone's Prosperity?"** Indeed, not every Country is Blest with the Necessary Mountains of Rocks for Building Beautiful Planned City States, which use Elevators, Escalators and Electric Subway Trains for Transportation, which are 99% Pollution-free. However, as True Christians, we can SHARE our Natural Resources with **"Seven Great Armies of Working Soldiers!" (HOW to Provide a Way for Everyone to WORK: so as to Eliminate Poverty, Crimes, Drug Abuses, Prisons and Unnecessary Taxes!) By The Worldwide People's Revolution!®**, Book 015, which is a Companion Book of: **"Poverty Hunger Riots Strikes Brutalities Election Deceptions and Civil Wars!" (The High Price that we Earthlings have Paid for Leaving the Good Land!) By The Worldwide People's Revolution!®**, Book 014, which is a Companion Book of: **"The Right Design for Living!" (A List of Great Advantages for Building Beautiful Planned City States!)**, Book 012, which is a Companion Book of: **"The IDEAL Place to Live!" (HOW to Discover an Ideal Place to Live!)**, Book 069, which is a Companion Book of: **"Our Elected King Who Speaks Out!" (It is High Time for some Sane Person to Get Control of this Insane World!) By The Worldwide People's Revolution!®** Book 070.

R-[_] I Fail to Understand all such Questions. The Thought is far too Deep for me to Understand. Therefore, I might have to be Recycled, just to Learn what it Means. In other Words, I might have to be Reincarnated in a more Miserable Place, just to Learn my Lessons, and thus Distinguish the Difference between GOOD and EVIL. Indeed, whatever Glorifies GOD is GOOD: beCause God is ALL that is Good, while Satan is ALL that is EVIL. Therefore, do not Credit God with Evil Inventions, lest you Offend him. ‡

S-[_] Satan is to be Blamed for all of our Troubles, who has Deceived us by Means of our own Witty Inventions — such as those Cars, Vans, Pickups, Trucks, Tractors, Buses, Bulldozers, Road Graders, Forklifts, Motorboats, Motorcycles, Motor Scooters, Noisy Lawnmowers, Stinking Chainsaws, Snow Blowers, Garden Tillers, and so on. Indeed, the City Bus is more Economical and less Polluting than 40 Cars for 40 Independent Jackasses; but, even the Bus is an Abomination in my Honest Opinion, even if it is an Electric Bus: beCause there is no Safe Place to Dispose of the Used Batteries, which are made of Poisonous and Dangerous Abominations. ‡

T-[_] I say that all such Things should be put on TRIAL, and Found Innocent or Guilty.

U-[_] You must Try to Understand that there is a much Better Way to Live, by Using Electric Elevators and Electric Subway Trains, which run on Direct Electricity from **Swanky Electric Generators,** which produce very little Pollution, and Avoid hundreds of Problems — such as Car Accidents, Insurance Bills, Pollutions, Taxes, and Endless Car Payments — all of which can be AVOIDED! After all, for the Costs of all such Vehicles, everyone could be Living in **"Beautiful Swanky PALACES!" (A New Concept in Living Habits — Swanky Palaces for Poor People!) By The Worldwide People's Revolution!®** Book 066. {See: **"The Low Court of Supreme Injustices is Brought to Trial!" (Our Elected King Butts Heads with the United States Supreme Court, with or without their Black Robes of Hypocrisies and Lies!) By The Worldwide People's Revolution!®**, Book 011, which Lists a hundred or more Reasons for going "Green."}

The Nature of CAPITALISM!

V-[_] Queen Victoria would Prefer that most People are Education Slaves, Work Slaves, Tax Slaves, Insurance Slaves, Interest Slaves, Rent Slaves, ElecTrickery Bills Slaves, Food Bills Slaves, Drug Slaves, Water Bills Slaves, Gas Bills Slaves, Childcare Bills Slaves, and Endless Bills Slaves. Indeed, it is the American Way. Therefore, it is GOOD. I Love it! §§

W-[_] We should not Judge any Subject, until after we have Learned ALL of the Evidences, lest we get ourselves into another Hateful World War: beCause of our Ignorance!

X-[_] X-amount of People do not have Enough Brains to Learn all such Lessons, much less Remember them. Indeed, they Desperately Need some Righteous King to Govern them, and tell them what is RIIT and WRong. (See: **"Thu Nq MAGNUFIID Verzhun uv Thu PROVERBZ uv KING SOLUMUN in Plaan Ingglish!"** (The Understandable Version of the Famous Proverbs of King Solomon in Plain English!) By The Worldwide People's Revolution!®, Book 028, which is a Companion Book of: **"ECCLESIASTES UNCOVERED!"** (The New MAGNIFIED Version of Ecclesiastes and the Song of Solomon in Plain English!), Book 034, which is a Companion Book of: **"The Process of Making a RIGHTEOUS KING!"** (A Fascination Autobiography of our Selected King!) By The Worldwide People's Revolution!®, Book 082, which is a Companion Book of: **"The New RIGHTEOUS One-World Government!"** (HOW to Establish a Righteous One-World Government without Going to WAR!) By The Worldwide People's Revolution!®, Book 056, which is a Companion Book of: **"The CONSTITUTION for the New RIGHTEOUS One-World GovernMINT!"** (HOW all People can Get True Justice, and Celebrate the Great Year of JUBILEE!), Book 016, which is a Companion Book of: **"The Great World TEMPLE of PEACE!"** (The Glory of Jerusalem Arises Again!) By The Worldwide People's Revolution!®, Book 017, which is a Companion Book of: **"The END of CONFUSION!"** (The Great CELEBRATION of the Magnificent Wedding of the Most-Humble Honest Nations, and the Grand Year of JUBILEE!) By The Worldwide People's Revolution!® Book 050. And some People Vainly Imagine that they already Know it ALL!}

Y-[_] That Kingship Nonsense was Good for Yesteryears, when most People were Extremely Ignorant, and had to have someone to Tell them what to Do; but, now, at this Time, no one has any Good Excuse for being Ignorant, much less being Murderers, who Drive Cars that Kill Innocent People by Various Means, Deliberately or not. †§‡

Z-[_] I Believe that the ZEAL of our Selected King will Deliver us from our MADNESS! After all, he Communicates with GOD, and can Answer all of our Important Questions. So, is that not the Work of GOD? [_] I say that it is, which is WHY that I Checked the Box.

{FOOTNOTE: See www.Amazon.com for: **"Are you a Jobless Graduate of the SKQL uv FQLZ?"** (HOW to get a GOUD EJUKAASHUN without Robbing the Bank!), Book 020, plus: **"The Public School of IGNERUNT FQLZ!"** (HOW we have been GRAATLEE DISEEVD by Capitalism!), Book 024, plus: **"Does a Good Soldier have to be a MURDERER?"** (Seven Great Swanky Armies of Voluntary Working Soldiers!), Book 027, plus: **"LIGHTNING STRIKES Versus Lightning Bugs!"** (HOW you can Become Moderately RICH, without Telling any Lies nor Selling any Trash!) By The Worldwide People's Revolution!®, Book

074, which also contains 2 very Enlightening Documents, called: **"WHO QUALIFIES to Rule Over US?"** and: **"The New MAGNIFIED Version of the 20 Commandments in Plain English!"** Surprise yourself!}

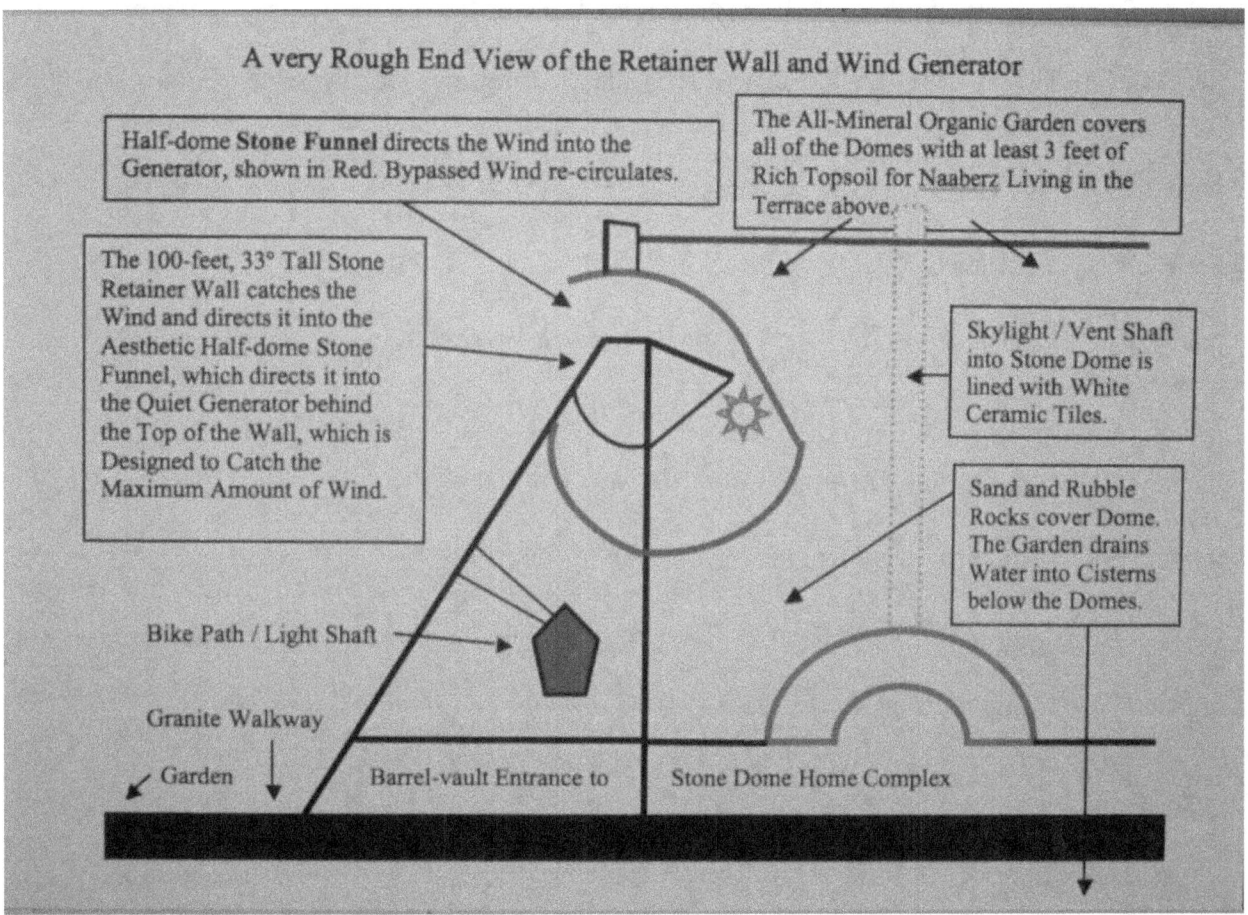

{Please Study the above Drawings, which Reveal HOW we can all have "Free" Electricity, once the Wind Generators are Set Up and Running. You can Prove this "Theory" to be Workable, just by going up to the Top of the Empire State Building in New York City, or to the Top of the Pyramid of the Sun in Mexico City, or to any High Hill or Mountain, and notice at the Crest of the Hill or Mountain, that the Wind is normally Blowing, and sometimes so Strong as to Blow Off your Hat! The Slanting Stone Wall could be 5, 10, 20, 50, or even 100 Miles Long, and surrounding a Beautiful Planned City State, whereby the Wind is Captured in the Arcade of Wind Funnels at the Tops of the Walls, which should be in Great Terraces, and as many as the People are Willing to Work for, according to **"A List of FAIR Swanky Wages,"** whereby they have an Abundance of Electricity throughout their Beautiful Planned City States. Indeed, every Educated Person knows that the Wind is always Blowing, somewhere, on the Great Plains, for Example, which is Begging us to Capture it and make it Useful, which is just one of the many Great Advantages for Building those **"GLORIOUS Swanky Hotels Castles and Fortresses!"** (Beautiful Planned City States for WISE Intelligent Well-Educated People with Common Sense and Good Understanding!) By The Worldwide People's Revolution!® Book 019.}

The Menu for a Spiritual Feast of Provable Truths

Chapter 01 — Just how GOOD are those Capitalist Cars? ... 13

Chapter 02 — How GOOD are those Wooden / Plastic Firetrap Mouse-infested Cockroach Dens? ... 22

Chapter 03 — The Evils of the Stock Market ... 25

Chapter 04 — Capitalism Destroyed the American Buffaloes ... 27

Chapter 05 — Capitalism is Responsible for Pollutions, Worldwide ... 29

Chapter 06 — How many Evils can be Attributed to Capitalism? ... 31

Chapter 07 — A Multitude of Little Capitalist Sins ... 38

Chapter 08 — Capitalists have Ruined the Water Supply ... 42

Chapter 09 — *"You shall Know them by their Fruits"* ... 45

Chapter 10 — Capitalist Lies by the Dozen! ... 48

Chapter 11 — The Power of Advertisements ... 50

Chapter 12 — Capitalism Produces Great STRESS! ... 54

Chapter 13 — Gambling with your Money or Life, is Routine with Capitalists ... 57

Chapter 14 — A Good Sermon from the Master Farmer ... 62

Chapter 15 — The Conclusion ... 67

A Short Photo Gallery for Capitalism … 71

A Long List of other Fascinating Literature by the same Inspired Author … 73

The Enticement is on the Inside of the Back Cover ... page 82

This Book contains Exactly 47,777 Words and 15 Black and White Photos with Explanations.

{FOOTNOTE: For Explanations of the Symbols (†§‡) that are used within this Book, see page 6, in: **"Was Billy Graham Greatly Deceived?" (Giving Honor to whom Honor is Due!) By The Worldwide People's Revolution!® Book 083.**}

(A List of the EVILS of CAPITALISM!)

— Chapter 01 —

Just how GOOD are those Capitalist Cars?

01-01 [_] If you are Seeking to Justify some Evil Thing, you must first of all BLOCK OUT any Truths that might Prove that Thing to be EVIL. For Example, everyone in his or her "RIIT Miind" must Confess that it would be Better to Spell "Right": R-I-I-T, than to spell it "W-r-i-g-h-t-w-e," or "r-i-g-h-t-e," as it used to be. Indeed, RIIT is Riit, being Simple and "EEZEE" for all Children to "LERN." However, Capitalism has much to Gain by making Words Difficult to SPELL, whereby Children must be FORCED to go to School, at the Expense of Tax Slaves, just to Learn HOW to "reed and riit." Likewise, CARS are very Profitable to a certain Class of Capitalists, including Insurance Agencies, who have raked in no less than a hundred Trillion Dollars from American Insurance Slaves, including Social Insecurity Taxes, who could have Spent that Money much more Wisely; but, only IF they were Educated with a Capital E, and Free with a Capital F, and Healthy with a Capital H, and Wise with a Capital W, and in Love with God with a Capital L, and "ONIST" with a Capital O — as in, "Oh my God, how many Lies must we Confess before we can be Liberated from this Prison of Lies with a Capital L?"

01-02 [_] O Selected King of **The Worldwide People's Revolution!®**, I will Confess right up front that you Live in another World, which I cannot Relate with. Yes, all such Thoughts are very Strange to me: beCause I have never Heard such Words before now. Are you an Alien, or what??

01-03 [_] Well, I am one of 7 Sons of a Righteous Man, who Believed in Free Enterprise, even as I also Believe; but, he was NOT a Greedy Selfish Capitalist HOG. Indeed, he only Wanted to Earn an Honest Living, even as everyone should; but, he had no Idea what "God's" Economic System would be Like: beCause, like those Hindus, who are not Taught anything about *The Book of MORMON*, he was not Taught anything about "SWANGKEENOMIKS," which Rules the Roost, as a Rooster might Crow at his Wedding, which is the Difference between Daylight and Dark, when it comes to Economics. In Fact, as far as I know, I am the ONE and ONLY American who ever HEARD of it, until NOW, when you have also just now Heard of it! Yes, it comes from 2 Words, namely: SWANKY and ECONOMICS, being spelled in "Funetik Ingglish," whereby a single Sound has a Single Way to Spell it. For Example, in Normal English, there are more than 20 Ways to Spell the single Sound of "OO" in: Sch**oo**l, d**o**, thr**ough**, sh**oe**, tw**o**, r**u**le, S**iou**x, L**ou**isiana, cr**ew**, bl**ue**, fr**ui**t, l**ieu**, rh**u**barb, rh**eu**matism, rondaavq, prooshqtoo, gql, and p**oo**h! Yes, "Q" is "OO" in Phonetic English. {See www.Amazon.com for: **"The New MAGNIFIED Version of The Book of MORMON!" (The Story of the White and Dark Indians in the Americas!) By The Worldwide People's Revolution!®** Book 040, Volumes 1 and 2, plus: **"SWANGKEENOMIKS Rules the Roost!" (HOW all People can Prosper in a RIIT WAA, and STOP Polluting the Earth with Capitalist TRASH!)**, Book 039, which is Greatly Enhanced by **"The New MAGNIFIED Version of the Book of ACTS!" (The Understandable Version of the ACTS of the Apostles in Plain English!)**, Book 063, which is Glorified by **"The New MAGNIFIED Version of the GOOD NEWS According to Saint LUKE!" (The Magnified Gospel of Luke in Plain English!) By The Worldwide People's Revolution!®**, Book 061, which makes it Possible to Understand what is Meant by having *"... all things in common among them."*}

01-04 [_] O Selected King, I Agree with you that we do have a LOT of Insane Traditions, that should be Revised or Eliminated; but, do you not even Appreciate the GOODNESS of Automobiles? Do you not Use them for Transportation? HOW could you Live without a CAR? Indeed, even Jesus Christ NEEDED a Stretched Limousine; but, he was Greatly Deprived of our American Blessings, which are Founded on the Consumption of ENERGY, which God has Abundantly Supplied in the Forms of Crude Oils, Natural Gases, Coals, Uranium, and whatever. Indeed, we have at least a hundred-year Supply of it left to Burn Up, which we can Speed Up by making Sure that everyone, except for Babies, have Vehicles to Drive. In Fact, I have a Hobby in my Garage, making Custom-made Cars; and I am now making one for the Time when Jesus Christ Returns in all of his Naked Glory in the Dark and Awesome Rolling Clouds of a FEARSOME Sky, along with his Holy Angels — each of whom will Need a New Car to Drive to Dizzy Land, in Californicate: so that they can go to the Water Park, and Play with Insanity Clauses. †§‡§§

01-05 [_] Well, like most People in the World, we have no Reasonable Options, now that "the BEAST" is in Total Control of the World. Therefore, I am FORCED to Use those Stinking Noisy Automobiles: beCause there are no Subway Electric Trains where I Live, whereby I might go down a Large Comfortable Solar-powered Electric Elevator, and get on the Swanky Electric Train with my Large Personal Shopping Cart, whereby I might Save X-amount of Energy: beCause Elevators and Trains are Extremely Efficient Means of Transportation. For Example, a Train can Travel on Level Tracks for only 2 Gallons of Diesel per Mile, even if the Train is 5 Miles Long — that is, once the Train gets Moving to its Maximum Speed of 40 Miles per Hour: beCause the Power is only needed to Push the Train through the Resisting AIR at the Head of it, and along the Sides of it, since the Wheels have very little Resistance to Overcome on a Level Track: beCause of being Well-Greased and Balanced. In Fact, there is not a more Efficient Way to Travel, than on an Electric Subway Train, which can be Designed to Build Up PRESSURE in Pressure Tanks as the Train is coming to a Stop, which Stored Energy can be Used Wisely to get the Train Moving Forward, once again, whereby much Energy can be Saved. Indeed, Energy is equally as Good as Money. {See www.Amazon.com for: **"UNLIMITED ENERJEE 99 Percent Pollutions Free!" (HOW to Obtain FREE ElecTrickery, Worldwide!), Book 029, plus: "The Right Design for Living!" (A List of Great Advantages for Building Beautiful Planned City States!), Book 012, plus: "GLORIOUS Swanky Hotels Castles and Fortresses!" (Beautiful Planned City States for WISE Intelligent Well-Educated People with Common Sense and Good Understanding!), Book 019, plus: "Seven Great Armies of Working Solders!" (HOW to Provide a Way for Everyone to WORK: so as to Eliminate Poverty, Crimes, Drug Abuses, Prisons and Unnecessary Taxes!) By The Worldwide People's Revolution!® Book 015.**}

01-06 [_] O Selected King, do you not Understand how STRESSED my Life is, without being Forced to "reed" all of those Books, even as Inspired as they might be?

01-07 [_] Well, my Inspired Books are Designed for a Lifetime of Education, Enlightenment, Entertainment, and Enjoyment. Therefore, if you are Stressed by the Thoughts of having to Study all of my Inspired Books within the next Day or 2, just RELAX: beCause there is no Way that you can Accomplish such a Thing within a Day or 2; but, within a Year or 2, you can Accomplish it. Guaranteed — that is, IF you have nothing else to Do. Yes, I have Proven it by Doing it, myself. Therefore, do not Fear it; but, be Persistent with it: beCause, if you are Deprived of the Best Books in the World, you are likely to Starve to Death for Spiritual Foods, even if you are Eating Enough to Feed a Walrus. {See the above Link for: **"DIETS!" (A Reasonable Solution for the "Eternal**

(A List of the EVILS of CAPITALISM!)

Controversy"!), Book 037, plus: "The Seven Basic Spiritual Building Blocks of LIFE!" (Faith, Hope, Trust, Love, Patience, Persistence and Obedience!) By The Worldwide People's Revolution!® Book 036.}

01-08 [_] So, O Selected King, are you Able to give to us a List of the EVILS of Cars, in Order to Persuade us that they are BAD?

01-09 [_] Well, I will now give to you such a List from A to Z, even though I will not go into all of the Gory Details: beCause I have no Desire to make everyone SICK by it; but, I do Want to Remind them of the EVILS of Capitalism. Please Check any Boxes with Statements that you Agree with, which will Help to Persuade you that Swangkeenomiks is a much Better Economic System. {See www.Amazon.com for: **"SWANGKEENOMIKS Rules the Roost!" (How all People can Prosper in a RIIT WAA, and STOP Polluting the Earth with Capitalist TRASH!) By The Worldwide People's Revolution!® Book 039.}**

A-[_] Car Accidents have Accounted for MILLIONS of Deaths during the past 100 Years, and BILLIONS of Injuries — Thanks to Capitalism, which is *"the Love of Money"* in Action, which did not Stop to Think about the EVILS that would Result from Making and Selling and Using CARS, Vans, Pickups, Trucks, Tractors, Buses, Motorcycles, etc.

01-[_] When a Car Accident takes place, even as several tens of thousands take place each Day, Worldwide, X-amount of People are Horrified and Grieved by it, even as Vice-President Joe Biden was Traumatized by the Death of his Wife, Years Ago, and yet he has not Mentioned the EVILS of Capitalism that CAUSED it: beCause of Seeking to Justify an Evil Economic System, which should be Trashed: beCause of being Ungodly, Unnecessary, Unsanitary, and Totally INSANE! ‡

02-[_] Car Accidents are often Extremely GORY Bloody Scenes, which make People SICK, just to Smell of the Blood and Spilled Guts.

03-[_] Medical Personnel in Ambulances Endanger their Lives, just to Rush to the Scenes of all such Crimes, who often Cause other Accidents.

04-[_] Medical Doctors are Forced against their Wills and Desires to Treat all such Wounded People, which Causes much Stress on them, which could be Avoided by not having Cars, Vans, Pickups, Trucks, Buses, Motorcycles, Motor Scooters, 4-Wheelers, nor even Airplanes, which are the Greatest Polluters. ‡

05-[_] Car Accidents often Cause Traffic Jams, which can Stretch Out for Miles, ..

A-[_] ... which Cause Stress in People who are just Naturally in a Hurry, ...

B-[_] ... which can Cause them to become ANGRY, ...

C-[_] ... which can Cause them to Do Strange Things, including Beating on their own Wives and Children when they finally get Home, ...

The Nature of CAPITALISM!

        01-[_] ... which can Cause a Whole List of Chain Reactions, ...

        02-[_] ... including Divorces, Murders, and whatever. {NOTE: You could fill a very large Book, bigger than the *Holy Bible,* with True Life Stories about the Evil Things that have Happened as a Direct or Indirect Result of Vehicular Accidents! Think of the many Musicians who have Died in all such Accidents. Remember John Denver, Ricky Nelson, Buddy Holly, Ritchie Valens, Jim Reeves, James Dean, and so on.}

B-[_] Car Accidents are often Involved with Train Wrecks, whereby Millions of Dollars are often Wasted, as well as much Time and Energy Cleaning Up the BIG Mess.

    01-[_] The Fire Department is often called after such Accidents: beCause the Cars often Catch on FIRE, ...

        A-[_] ... which can Cause Prairie Fires, Forest Fires, House Fires, etc., etc.

        B-[_] ... which can Cause an entire List of Evils, as a Result of just one Car Accident.

        C-[_] For Example, a Policeman was the first to Arrive at a certain Car Accident, and saw that the Lady inside of the Car was about to Burn Up Alive; and therefore, he Instinctively reached out to Open the Car Door, which Burned his Hands so Severely that he missed a Month of Work, ...

            01-[_] ... which Caused him to Miss Paying his Bills, ...

                A-[_] ... which Caused a whole List of Evils, and ended with a Divorce! ...

                B-[_] ... which Ended when he Committed Suicide!

C-[_] People have been known to Back Out of their Garages with their Cars, and Run Over their own Children, or the Naaber Children, whereby another whole List of Evils followed such Grievous Things: beCause of being Related with MURDER, ...

    01-[_] ... whereby the "Murderer" has rarely Forgiven him or herself, ...

        A-[_] ... whereby he or she has gone into a State of Depression, ...

            01-[_] ... whereby a whole List of Evils have Followed it with Chain Reactions that Affected many Families in a Bad Way.

    02-[_] ... whereby GUILT has Driven such People Insane: beCause of their Racked Consciences, ...

(A List of the EVILS of CAPITALISM!)

A-[_] ... which have Led to Overeating, Bad Health, Drunkenness, Drugs, Doctor Bills, Hospital Bills, Arguments, Fights, etc., etc.

D-[_] Trash Dumps are filled with Used Oil Cans and Plastic Bottles and other Trash from Car Repair Shops, which would not be the Case, if we were all Living in: **"GLORIOUS Swanky Hotels Castles and Fortresses!" (Beautiful Planned City States of WISE Intelligent Well-Educated People with Common Sense and Good Understanding!)**, Book 019.

01-[_] Those Used Oil Cans and Bottles often contain Oils, which Pollute the Land and Water, and thus Cause another whole List of the Evils of Capitalism.

02-[_] Used Motor Oil is often Dumped Down Toilet Drains, directly into the Sewage System, whereby the Sewage is Greatly Polluted, which could otherwise be used for Fertilizer on Hay Fields, or in Forests.

E-[_] Cars are Painted with Highly Toxic Abominable Paints, which Pollute the World, and Cause Cancers, Respiratory Diseases, and who knows what else? (See *Silent Spring*.)

F-[_] Children have been known to Drink Anti-Freeze, and thus Kill themselves — Thanks to Automobiles.

G-[_] Garages are Stinking Filthy Greasy Places, all around the World, which Stink in the Nostrils of God and of his Holy Angels.

H-[_] Hospitals are full of People with Lung Diseases: beCause of Breathing the Bad Air, which is Produced by Burning Gases in Automobiles, Trucks, Buses, etc.

01-[_] Another whole List of Evils must Follow the above Fact: beCause of Patients being "Treated" with MediSINZ, which Produce their own Long List of Capitalist Evils, whereby People Suffer with more than a MILLION Diseases — most of which are Related with the Use of Cars, Tractors, Pesticides, Herbicides, Drugs, Preservatives in Foods, and whatever Abominations that Capitalists can come up with for making a "Profit."

02-[_] Medical Doctors Know for a Fact that Gasoline-powered Vehicles are no Good; but, they are Forced by the Great False Economy to be HYPOCRITES. Indeed, they cannot even Speak Evil of that which is Evil: beCause they also Use those Abominations, just to get to Work.

I-[_] Industries around the World are Dependent on the Use of Motorized Vehicles, which are always in Danger of becoming Obsolete: beCause of someone Inventing a "Better Abomination." But, when we "Bild" those Beautiful Planned City States, all such Industries are almost Guaranteed to go Out of "Biznus": beCause of becoming Obsolete.

J-[_] Junkyards are full of Trashed Cars, which Junkyards are Notoriously UGLY Sites, which are Numbered in the hundreds of thousands, Worldwide, which People try to Hide behind Trees, Bushes, and Tall Ugly Rusty Capitalist Tin Walls: beCause a Good Stone Wall would Cost too much, which brings up another whole List of the Evils that are brought about by a Lack of Money, which alone could Fill an entire Book! Just Think of the Silly Things that you have done during your Life for a Lack of MONEY!

> 01-[_] For Example, for a Lack of Money, Capitalists cannot Afford to Fix the Highways, Bridges, Drainage Systems, and whatever has "gone to Hell," or is presently going to Hell, as they say.

> 02-[_] Pot Holes in the Highways Damage the Vehicles, which Cause another Long List of Capitalist Evils, which are Paid for by the Duped Believers in Capitalism, who were never Taught anything about a Better Way to Live, who do not even Believe that there IS a Better Way to Live: beCause they have only ever Heard of 3 Ways to Lives — namely by Means of Capitalism, Communism, or Socialism: beCause Swangkeenomiks is never Mentioned in the Publik Skql uv Ignerunt Fqlz.

K-[_] Many Kingdoms have come and gone; but, the most Evil of them has been the Capitalist Empire, which has Contaminated the Air, Water, and Land beyond Measure: beCause no one Knows just how MUCH Damage has already been Done by Using Cars, Vans, Pickups, Trucks, Buses, Bulldozers, Road Graders, Tractors, Combines, Motorboats, Motorcycles, Motor Scooters, 4-Wheelers, Weed-eaters, Grass Trimmers, Garden Tillers, Lawnmowers, Hedge Trimmers, Snow Blowers, Snowmobiles, Chainsaws, Forklifts, and all Kinds of Gasoline-powered Machines — such as Concrete Mixers and Shredders.

L-[_] Because of those Greasy Vehicles, much Laundry Detergents have been Used by Ignorant People, who have Contaminated the Lands, Rivers, Lakes, Seas, and Oceans.

M-[_] Mobile Homes have Costed Americans Billions of Dollars: beCause of being Destroyed by Tornadoes, Floods, Fires, and whatever; and all of them are Destined for the Trash Dumps: beCause of being First Class Inventions of Capitalists, who saw a Way to Rob Poor People, who could not Afford Good Houses, which are Beautiful Stone Dome Homes, which are Self-air-conditioned, Fireproof, Mouse-proof, Termite-proof, Rot-proof, Paint-proof, Tornado-proof, Hurricane-proof, Flood-damage-proof, Insurance-proof, and would be Tax-proof, if I were the Elected King of **"The New RIGHTEOUS One-World Government!" (HOW to Establish a Righteous One-World Government without Going to WAR!) By The Worldwide People's Revolution!® Book 056.**

> 01-[_] And that brings up another Long List of the Evils of Capitalism, which I will go into Details on, later on, ...

> 02-[_] ... which is a Waste of my Precious Time to make such Lists, and a Waste of your Time to read them — except that you probably never Heard about the EVILS of Capitalism, until NOW.

N-[_] Not everyone can Afford to Buy a Car, much less a "Good" Car; and therefore, millions of Old Badly-running Cars are Sold to Poor People, who are Guilt-ridden for Polluting the Earth — NOT beCause they Want to Pollute the Earth; but, beCause they

(A List of the EVILS of CAPITALISM!)

have no Idea HOW to "Prosper" without Buying a Car, Pickup, Van, Motorcycle, or whatever they Need to Transport themselves to Work in the City of Confusion; or, to just Haul their Fruits and Vegetables to Town, to Sell: beCause of Living on Farms.

    01-[_] And that brings up another whole List of the Evils of Capitalism, whereby little Gardeners and Farmers are Forever Stuck in their States of Poverty, whose Barnyards are Overrun with Used Vehicles, which Broke Down or Wore Out.

    02-[_] And that brings up another whole List of Capitalist Repair Bills: beCause all of those Farm Tools are Designed to Endure until the Guarantees Expire, and then they Need Costly Repairs, which can Cost half as much as a New Car: beCause Tractors are made of Special Parts, and no Junkyard Parts will Fit the Newer Tractors: beCause there are 240 Billion Different Models of Tractors, Trucks, Pickups, Vans, Buses, Trucks, Cars, Airplanes, Boats, Engines, etc., etc.

O-[_] Capitalism Offers OPTIONS by the Millions: beCause it is much more Profitable than having just ONE Really GOOD Tractor, Car, Pickup, Truck, Bus, or whatever, whereby all Parts are Interchangeable and Reusable. Indeed, if there were only ONE Good Car Engine, you could possible get a nearly New Used Engine for half the Price: beCause of those Car Accidents; but, now you have to Buy a New Car: beCause the Engine, alone, would Cost half as much as a New Car, whose Seats are already Worn Out!

P-[_] Car Parts Stores are everywhere, and there are BILLIONS of Parts; but, not for your 1911 Silver Queen Rolls-Royce: beCause it is "Obsolete," in spite of running well. Indeed, it only Needs a 10$ Part to Fix it; but, none of those Parts Stores have the Part you Need: beCause no Extra Parts were made for your 1911 Silver Queen Rolls-Royce: beCause it was Designed to Run "FOREVER"! In Fact, the Silver Queen that Won the World Race in 1911 is still Running on the same Engine! (See *Wikipedia* for the Proof.)

Q-[_] The Old Antique Cars can be Repaired, if you are Skilled enough to Manufacture your own Parts, and do whatever Work is Necessary to Repair them; but, Thanks to Capitalism, they do not Meet Modern Environmental Standards, whereby they are not Legal to Drive in certain Cities, which can Cause you to be Fined for Driving there, which can Cause you to get Pissed Off, as they say, and even Want to Kill the Copperhead who Arrests you for it, and Knees you in the Groin at the Police Station for Sassing him.

R-[_] Cars have been Used as Weapons to Kill People who have Gathered in Crowds, which would be Impossible within a Swanky Fortress, which is Designed for Living in Peace, without any Cars: beCause they use Elevators and Electric Subway Trains.

S-[_] Stinking Polluting Cars have often been used for Committing Suicide, by Running a Vacuum Cleaner Hose from the Exhaust Pipe into the Rear Side Window of those Cars, which is one of the more Popular Ways for Capitalists to get "Revenge" on Capitalism. §§

T-[_] Millions of Tons of Waste Products have been Produced while Refining Crude Oils — such as the Tar Sands Oil from Canada, which everyone Wants Buried in his or her own Front Yard: so as to be Able to Enjoy the Toxic Fumes that Arise Eternally into the Nostrils of the Gods, who Created all such Evil Things, just to Test our Souls for our Goodness, and then Commanded us, saying: *"Come Out from among the Wicked Ones, O my People, and Separate yourselves from them, and Touch NONE of their Unclean Filthy Stinking Things, lest you become Partakers of their Sins, whereby you shall be Destroyed with them. Yes, Remember Lot's Wife, and do not Look Back with Lingering Desires to Return like a Dog to Eat his own Vomit; but, be you HOLY, even as I am Holy, and Live in Beautiful Planned City States, which are Designed for True Prosperity."* — The Good News According to our Elected King, which God Authorizes. (See *Second Corinthians 6—7:1*.)

U-[_] Universities have Wasted Millions of Dollars on Worthless Experiments for Unneeded Electric Cars, which Time and Money could have been Spent much more Wisely on the Construction of a Swanky Fortress, as well as the Trillions of Dollars that have been Wasted on so-called "good educations," but, without a Capital G nor E: beCause they are Actually very "Bad Educations," which are so BAD that none of the Professors can Present even ONE Great Disadvantage for Building and Living within a Swanky Fortress, which has NO Traffic Jams, NO Car Accidents, NO Pollution from Spilled Motor Oil, Gas, and other Poisonous Fluids from Cars, Van, Pickups, Trucks, Buses, Tractors, Bulldozers, Road Graders, Motorboats, Motorcycles, Motor Scooters, Lawnmowers, Chainsaws, Snow Blowers, and Airplanes.

V-[_] Vehicles are Famous for Running Over Pedestrians, and Killing or Wounding them, which has never Happened at a Swanky Hotel, Castle, nor Fortress in all of History: beCause they have no Need for such Abominations; and everyone can Live in **"Beautiful Swanky PALACES,"** which I have Described in: **"The Environmentalists' Paradise!" (HOW almost Everyone could be Living in a Beautiful Manmade Paradise!) By The Worldwide People's Revolution!®** Book 035.

W-[_] Horses and Wagons may Run Over you, and even Kill you; but, no one Needs any such Vehicles, nowadays: beCause we have Electric Elevators and Trains, which are much more Efficient. However, it could be Argued that it was beCAUSE of Horses and Wagons that Cars, Vans, Pickups, Trucks, Buses, and all such Evil Things were Invented: beCause People Needed Vehicles to Transport their Goods all about. However, if they had Stopped to THINK, they might have Thought of those **"GLORIOUS Swanky Hotels Castles and Fortresses!" (Beautiful Planned City States for WISE Intelligent Well-Educated People with Common Sense and Good Understanding!)**, Book 019, which have more than 5,000 Good Reasons and Great Advantages for Building them and Living within the Borders of them! {See www.Amazon.com for: **"The Low Court of Supreme Injustices is Brought to Trial!" (Our Elected King Butts Heads with the United States Supreme Court, with or without their Black Robes of Hypocrisies and Lies!), Book 011, plus: "A Sure Cure for GUN VIOLENCE!" (HOW TO STOP GANG WARS and CRIMINAL SHOOTINGS!), Book 031, plus: "The Right Design for Living!" (A List of Great Advantages for Building Beautiful Planned City States!) By The Worldwide People's Revolution!®** Book 012.}

X-[_] X-amount of Americans have already Wasted X-amount of TRILLIONS of Dollars on Cars, Gas, Oil, Insurance, Repairs, Cleaning, Waxing, Polishing, and Transporting Cars, which could have been Spent much more Wisely by Building those Beautiful Planned City

(A List of the EVILS of CAPITALISM!)

States, which have no Need for Cars, Buses, Tractors, nor other Abominations: beCause of being Properly DESIGNED for True Prosperity. However, if Americans had Spent that much Time, Money, Materials, and Energy, and they were all Healthy, Wealthy, and WISE, I would be the Last to Complain about it! But, being 147 Trillion Dollars in DEBT to those Greedy Edomite Banksters, I must Confess that our Forefathers had a very BAD VISION of how Things should be, who Instituted the EVIL Stock Market, which made it Possible for People to Produce all such Abominations as Cars, Vans, Pickups, Trucks, Buses, Motorboats, Motorcycles, Lawnmowers, Chainsaws, and whatever the Baby Jesus Lived Happily without! (NOTE: I Hear Capitalist Heads EXPLODING after Hearing those Words, which I will Address later.)

Y-[_] Car Dealers are no doubt Yearning for the Day when they go Out of Business, whereby they can Stop Lying about the Goodness of their Vehicles. §

Z-[_] The Great ZEAL to Produce more and more Vehicles, even by the Chinese, has brought about Radical Climate Changes, according to Top Scientists, who seem to be Equally as Puzzled as Politicians for Reasonable Solutions: beCause they have not Thought about those **"GLORIOUS Swanky Hotels Castles and Fortresses!"** Indeed, the very Idea, even now, FRIGHTENS them: beCause they might also be put OUT of Business! After all, once those Swanky Fortresses are Built, there will be very little Need for 90% or more of those so-called "Scientists," who will simply have to Retire with those Politicians, Preachers, Teachers, Professors, Chemists, Medical Doctors, Insurance Agents, Bankers, Lawyers, Judges, and whomever Fights Against **"The Swanky Sword of Divine Truths!" (The Most Powerful Weapon in the Whole Universe!) By The Worldwide People's Revolution!®**, Book 067: beCause the KING of Kings will have no Use for them! In Fact, if they were Wise, they would Learn to be Good Honest Botanists, Architects, Engineers, Stone Masons, and Useful People. {See www.Amazon.com for: **"How to Prepare for CLIMATE CHANGES!" (The Wisest Plan for Mankind to Follow!) By The Worldwide People's Revolution!® Book 004.**}

01-10 [_] Okay, O Elected King of the Mountains, I am Satisfied that almost all Vehicles are BAD; and therefore, I am now Wishing to God that I had never Mentioned making any List of the EVILS of Cars: because it is Obvious that there are many Bad Chain Reactions, which alone could possibly fill a boring book, which no American would be Interested in reading. In Fact, it is Doubtful that most Americans will be Able to Persuade themselves to read this one Chapter, let along the Remainder of this Book, which is not just Hypercritical, without any Reasonable Solutions: beCause I could not Resist the Great Temptation to SKIP Forward, and Discover what some of those Solutions are, which make me Feel like a FOOL for Doubting your Master Plan, which is Actually quite Reasonable, and much Better than anything that those Dimwitcrats and Reprobates in Washington have to Offer, who do not even know how to Prevent the Common Cold! {See the above Link for: **"Did God or Satan Ordain Medical Doctors??" (Ask Huck Finn and/or Nigger Jim: because neither Tom Sawyer nor Judge Thatcher would Know!)**, Book 022, plus: **"The BIG White OUTHOUSE on the Not-so-Biblical Capitol DUNGHILL!" (The Chief Sins of the Divided States of United Lies!) By The Worldwide People's Revolution!® Book 023.**}

— Chapter 02 —

How GOOD are those Capitalist Wooden / Plastic Firetrap Mouse-infested Cockroach Dens?

02-01 [_] The "American Dream" is to OWN one of those almost Worthless Houses, if you can Believe it! Yes, here is their Plan:

A-[_] When you are Young, and perhaps have just Graduated from College, being 40,000$ or more in Debt for the College Loans, you first must go to a Friendly Banker, who puts out his Right Hand of "Christian Fellowship," and Welcomes you into his Trap with a BIG Smile, and says: "How may I Help you, my Son?" (He should say, "How may I ROB you, O Ignorant Education Slave, who is about to become an Interest / Usury Slave?")

B-[_] Then, without any Awareness that it is a Special Educated and Calculated Trap, you Boldly Confess that you Need enough Money to Buy an "American Dream Home," even if it Requires 40 Years or more to Pay Off the Loan. After all, this Agreement is "Life in Prison as an Interest / Usury Slave," and without any Relief: beCause, if you Fail to make only one or 2 Payments on your Loan / Debt, you could Lose the entire House! (At least that was the American Way for the first 250 Years, even if it is presently Modified to Accommodate an "Extended Loan" with "Low Interest Rates" — Thanks to Government Regulations, which did not take Effect until after MILLIONS of People Lost their Homes during "the Great Recession," which Euphemistically Describes it.)

C-[_] You must Present Proof to the Friendly Banker that you have a JOB, even if it is only Washing Dishes at a Restaurant at Minimum Wages, or Painting those Wooden Houses, whereby you can Fill your Head and Lungs with the Paint Fumes, which is like going to Satan's Heaven, where there are Countless Drugs, Solvents, Paint Thinners, Glues, and Evil Things to SNIFF.

D-[_] Then, if all goes Well, you can Sweat Out the "Eternal Debt," which, of course, is much Better than Living in a Used Rusty Van down by the River with "Nigger Jim" and Huck Finn. After all, you do Live in "the Greatest Nation on Earth," which is only 147 Trillion Dollars in DEBT, with no Guarantee that you will be Able to Collect your Social Insecurity Check when you get ready to Retire at 84 Years of Age — that is, IF you make it there, after Paying in some 300,000$ for Social Security Insurance (SSI). Indeed, there are some 20,000+ People Living in the Sewage Systems and Subways of American Cities of Confusion: beCause of what they call "Burn Out." †§‡

E-[_] Yes, it might all be Funny, if you could not Think, nor Remember anything; but, behold, you never know just WHEN the Great False Economy will have another Great Recession, or even another Great Depression, and much Worse than Americans and Europeans Suffered during the 1930's — that is, except for Germany, who Voted for Adolf Hitler, who got Germany OUT of the Great Depression within 6 Months, after getting into

(A List of the EVILS of CAPITALISM!)

Total Control, and Built Up the Greatest Army that ever Patrolled the Earth! Yes, he got so Bold as to Attempt to Conquer Capitalism and Communism with National German Socialism, which almost Worked, and probably would have Worked, if Albert Einstein had not Defected, and Moved to America! Yes, Hitler had Access to only 5% of the World's Natural Resources, while the Capitalists and Communists had the other 95%, and yet they almost LOST the War: beCause, like the Southern States, those Germans were Inspired by a "JUST CAUSE" for going to War, while the Americans, Brits and Russians were only Playing a Normal War Game, without any Justified Cause, except to Defend the Bankers: beCause they have always LOVED those Wars, ever since God can Remember, while the Germans just Naturally Hated those Wars, and did everything Humanly Possible to AVOID them, which is WHY Hitler BEGGED American, French and British Officials to have a Meeting with him, rather than go to War; but, they Refused to Meet — even as George Warmonger Bush Refused to Meet with Saddam Hussein, in Iraq, before Wasting 2 Trillion Dollars and Millions of Lives! Yes, you might Recall that GREAT Britain had a Great Empire, after Conquering many Nations, including China and India, while the Spaniards Conquered most of Central and South America; but, Germans never did set out to Conquer the World, as some Silly People might Vainly Imagine. Indeed, Adolf was only Attempting to put the German Empire in Europe back Together again, which consisted of Germany, Austria, Czechoslovakia, the Kingdom of Prussia, Hungary, the Ottoman Empire, Bulgaria, Ukraine, Poland, Lithuania, Netherlands, Switzerland, and so on — all of which were Basically Germans. †§‡

F-[_] And now, 40 Years Later, and 3 Mortgages Later, you still do not Actually OWN your "All-American Dream Home": beCause it still Belongs to that Friendly Banker, who has Collected no less than 300,000$ for Interest or Usury on the Loan for a 120,000$ House (which might Sell for only 20,000$), plus Insurance for no less than another 100,000$, for a Total of about 520,000 Dollars, which makes you HAPPY! Yes, that is WHY you can See so many Smiling Faces in Bar Rooms and at Churches: beCause they are DRUGGED with the Opium of Stupidity and Regret! After all, for 520,000$, you could have Built a Swanky Stone Dome Home Complex worth no less than 3 Million Dollars, and had NO Insurance Bills, Heating, nor Cooling Bills, at all! But, the School of Fools did not Explain all of that to you: beCause they wanted you to have a GOOD education without a Capital G nor E. In Fact, what they Wanted to do was to make you and everyone else into a Future Education Slave, Work Slave, Interest Slave, Tax Slave, Drug Slave, Sex Slave, Insurance Slave, and Endless Bills Slave; but, without a Direct Visible Slave Master with a Whip in his Hand: beCause there is more than one Way to make People into SLAVES. †§‡

G-[_] Meanwhile, that "Precious House" will Require thousands of dollars-worth of Repairs: beCause it is Designed Perfectly for that, which will Cost an Average of at least 1,000$ per Year, even if you do not Change the Carpet every Year or 2, as some People do, who have more Money than Brains, who do not know that Granite Tiles are Cheaper in the Long Run, and Marble Walls are Cheaper than Painted Walls; but, only IF the Polished Marble is placed on Solid Mouse-proof Rot-proof Termite-proof Concrete or Stone Walls, which, of course, you could never Afford, unless you were RICH; and the Government and Bankers will always Work Hand-in-Hand to make SURE that you never get "Truly Rich," unless you want to Play in the Grand Casino on Wall Street, called the Stock Market, where you are just as apt to Lose as Win. After all, for every "Winner," there are a thousand Losers! But, the School of Fools never mentions that Fact. ‡

H-[_] Nevertheless, you can now be Happy: beCause a Tornado or Fire could have Wiped you Out, and left you Homeless, like those People in the Subways and Under Bridges and in Culverts under Highways, where they can Comfort themselves with the "Music" of the Traffic passing by overhead.

02-02 [_] O Selected King, are you not being very Pessimistic? — and maybe too Pessimistic for your own Good? After all, you are "Picking" on almost all of us Americans, who Live in such Firetrap Mouse-infected Cockroach Dens.

02-03 [_] Well, it might seem like I am being too Pessimistic, whereby I will be making X-amount of Enemies; but, it is just a Matter of Time, and none of those Houses will be Worth anything: beCause all such Cities will be Abandoned and Forsaken and Forgotten: beCause most People will become Wiser than they now are, and will Decide to Submit to **"The Swanky Sword of Divine Truths,"** and Move into Swanky Fortresses: beCause of the 5,000+ Good Reasons and Great Advantages for Building them and Living within the Borders of them, including Safe Places to Live, even if the Terrorists get as THICK as Cat Hairs Outside of those Fortresses. ‡

02-04 [_] So, O Elected King, if the Cities of Confusion are Abandoned, WHO will Pay the Taxes for Paying Off our National, State, County, and City Debts?

02-05 [_] Well, all such Debts will have to be Forgiven, which will take Care of that Problem, Worldwide. (See *Leviticus 25*.)

02-06 [_] So, O Elected King, do you Sincerely Believe that those Greedy Selfish Red Jew Bankers will Actually Forgive ALL Debts?

02-07 [_] Well, they can Collect all of the Wooden / Plastic Firetrap Houses that they might Want, if the Ashes have not Washed Away. After all, there will hardly be any Options at that Time: beCause they will not be Able to get Blood from Turnips, as the saying goes. Indeed, they are the Unholy Ones who Set Up the Disaster, and would not Loan Money for Building GOOD Houses. Therefore, what can they Expect with such a Great False Economy? ‡

02-08 [_] So, O Elected King, it Sounds as if the Prophecies in *the Book of Revelation* could Actually Happen, huh?

02-09 [_] Well, that is the Way it Appears to be.

02-10 [_] So, O Elected King, what about the Evils of the Stock Market? Are they all that Bad?

— Chapter 03 —

The Evils of the Stock Market

03-01 [_] Most People do not Realize that the single most Vile Thing in this World, in the Eyes of God, is the Stock Market: beCause it makes it Possible for Abominations — such as Cars, Vans, Trucks, Buses, Motorcycles, Motorboats, Lawnmowers, Chainsaws, Cokes, Cigarettes, Candies, Cookies, Cakes, Pies, Poisonous Beers, Poisoned Wines, Poisoned Bananas, Poisoned Apples, Poisoned Oranges, and whatever else — to be SOLD: beCause Capitalism does not Care whether or not you Live or Die, just as long as it gets "RICH" by Selling those Things — even if those are the FALSE Riches. Indeed, the Stock Market makes it Possible for almost anyone to Invent in and Sell some Abomination: beCause the "Investors" Visualize the Potential of all such Products; and thereby they Buy Stocks and Bonds to Promote the Production and Sales of all such EVIL Products. But, they do not have a Dime to Invest in Swanky Fortresses: beCause those Fortresses would put them OUT of Business! Guaranteed! ‡

03-02 [_] For Example, when George Washington started growing Tobacco to Sell to the British Drug Addicts, he listened to the "Good Advice" of his Secretary of the Treasury, Alexander Hamilton, and together, they got the New York Stock Exchange in Operation, which is presently the World's Largest Stock Exchange with some 20 Trillion Dollars in "Securities." George was the Richest American, who Sold Tobacco, Whiskey, and other Drugs: beCause that is where the Big Money was. After all, if you are going to get into a Capitalist Business, you might as well get into one that is Profitable above all others, and that is something that People can get ADDICTED to, whereby they must Keep Buying more of it, which, in his Case was Tobacco and Whiskey — both of which Stored Well for Years, which made it Ideal for Shipping across the Great Ocean of Future Filthiness, being the Disposal Dump for BILLIONS of Gallons of Toxic Wastes, as if it were a Proper Sewage System for Mankind. Therefore, when "Investors" saw that Tobacco was Selling Well in Europe, they just Naturally Wanted some of the "Profits," which was made Possible by Buying Stocks in Tobacco Industries! And thus we have a handful of very Rich Capitalists, who Sell Tobacco Products to Billions of very Poor Miserable Addicted FOOLS, who are almost Guaranteed to Contract Cancers, Lung Diseases, and who knows what else — all beCause of the "Wonderful and Marvelous" Stock Exchange, which can also CRASH! †§‡

03-03 [_] Indeed, you can read about the Great Depression during the 1930's, when thousands of those "Investors" contemplated Suicide, and some of them went through with it: beCause of Losing everything they had: beCause the Stock Exchange is a Legal Gambling Game on Wall Street, while **"SWANGKEENOMIKS Rules the Roost!" (How all People can Prosper in a RIIT WAA, and STOP Polluting the Earth with CAPITALIST TRASH!)**, Book 039, is no Gamble at all: beCause it is a Foolproof Economic System, whereby every Honest Hardworking Person in the World is Guaranteed to become Moderately RICH with the True Riches, beginning with Good Health, which apparently never crossed the Minds of General George President Washington, Thomas Inventor Jefferson, nor Alexander Dueling Hamilton, who was a War Hero, who took one Last Gamble with his Life, and Lost!

03-04 [_] So, O Selected King, are you saying that God HATES the Stock Market, just beCause a few Not-so-Wise Investors Buy the WRong Stocks, or what??

03-05 [_] No. I am saying that God Hates the Stock Market for the EVILS that it Produces — such as Promoting the Selling of Drugs, Polluting Automobiles, Cokes, Candies, Cookies, Chips, Dips, and other Addictive Foods and Drinks, which have Caused Americans and even Non-Americans to become EXCESSIVELY FAT, which is not GOOD: beCause those Obese People are a Great Burden on the Backs of Tax Slaves and Insurance Slaves. Indeed, I call them "the Victims of Capitalism": beCause they have been Sold BAD Things, which are Advertised on Radio and TV, Incessantly, as if People Needed all such Evil Things to be Happy! Yes, it is like getting Drunk, which, at first, seems to be "Funny," which is why Beer is often called "Happy Water": beCause it seems to make People Happy; but, too much "Happiness" can get a Person into a Mortuary, just by Driving a Car after getting Drunk, which seems to be BAD to me; but, NOT to the Federal Government, which has no Limit on how much a Fool should be Allowed to Drink: beCause that would be Depriving that Ignorant Fool of his or her FREEDOMS, if they were Limited by some Tyrannical Government! Indeed, it might not be so Bad, IF such a Drunkard did not have a Vehicle to Murder some other Innocent People with. However, in **"The Divided States of United Lies!" (The so-called "United States of North America" in Disguise!)**, Book 058, X-amount of Victims of Capitalism get Killed each Year — all for the Lack of some WISDOM, which is Free!

03-06 [_] So, O Elected King, do you Suggest that we SEPARATE the "Good People" from the "Bad People": so that Good Law-abiding People cannot be Taxed for Supporting the Lawbreakers?

03-07 [_] Yes, that is what I Recommend. However, more than that, I Suggest that we Separate them into Religious and Political Groups, where they have Total Freedom to Govern themselves, according to their own Elected Laws and Flexible Rules: so that no one can Complain about not having their "Freedoms" to Sin, if that is what they Choose to Do. In other Words, the Smokers would have to Live with other Smokers in Present-day Cities of Confusion: beCause, **"The New RIGHTEOUS One-World Government"** would NOT Assist them to Build Beautiful Planned City States for themselves; but, it would Assist all of the Righteous People to Do that: beCause they are Worthy of Living without all such Taxes, Insurance, Interest on Loans, and so on. †‡

03-08 [_] O Selected King, if the Government Assisted the Righteous People to get Moderately Rich, the Wicked People would become Poorer and POORER: beCause of having to Tax themselves more and more, just to Manage the Criminals that they would Produce. In Fact, those Cities of Confusion would be Regular Hell Holes, you might say: beCause even the Righteous Policemen, Lawyers, Judges, Teachers, and Honest People would LEAVE, and Move into those **"GLORIOUS Swanky Hotels Castles and Fortresses!" (Beautiful Planned City State for WISE Intelligent Well-Educated People with Common Sense and Good Understanding!)**, Book 019, which would be Good for them; but, not at all Good for the Disobedient People, Thieves, Liars, Hypocrites, Politicians, Medical Doctors, and other Snakes and Criminals like Bernie Madoff and those Hateful TERRORISTS! ‡

03-09 [_] And what would be so BAD about that?

03-10 [_] Well, it would no doubt Cause the Stock Market to Permanently CRASH, whereby most Rich People would be BROKE, and then they would not have any Money for Charity, if you know what I Mean. Indeed, they would not have any Money for Cancer Research and other very Worthy Endeavors — such as going to Mars and Venus: beCause, **"The New RIGHTEOUS One-World Government"** would Certainly NOT be Interested in any such Worthless Nonsense! †§‡

(A List of the EVILS of CAPITALISM!)

— Chapter 04 —

Capitalism Destroyed the American Buffaloes

04-01 [_] Now we are Addressing a Major Crime: beCause the American Bisons were the "Caretakers of the Great Plains," who Planted the Seeds of the Tall Grasses in the Deep Rich Topsoil, which Required the WEIGHT of the Buffaloes, just to PUSH DOWN the Seeds Deep enough into the Mat of Grassroots, in Order to make them Sprout and Grow Well: beCause the Topsoil had a THICK MAT of Roots, 2 feet Deep, which Quickly Absorbed any Heavy Rains, which Prevented Flooding in the Rivers, which Flooding now Costs Americans an Average of Billions of Dollars per Year for Levees and Repairs for Houses and whatever — Thanks to Capitalism and "Free Enterprise," whereby X-amount of "Farmers" and "Ranchers" put Fences around their Properties, and proceeded to "Run" Livestock, whereby they Overgrazed the Land, Plowed Away the Tall Grasses, and made an Unnatural DISASTER of the Not-so-Great Plains, which "Farming" eventually Transformed it into a Giant DUST BOWL, which was Blowing Dust all of the Way to Kentucky and West Virginia, which was sometimes so Thick with Dust in Brokelahoma, Kansas, Nebraska, North Dakota, and Texas, that a Farmer could not See his own Hands at Arms-length, and his own Bed was Covered with a Quarter of an Inch of Dust, each Morning: beCause of the Dust Seeping through the Cracks around the Widows and Doors of his Firetrap Mouse-infested Rat-infested House. (My Grandfather would follow a Rope that led to the Barn Door, whereby he might Milk his Cow, and Feed his Chickens, who Stopped Laying Eggs and Stopped Producing Milk within a couple of Months of that Mistreatment: beCause of the Dust in their Eyes. The Wooden Barn Walls were full of Leaking Cracks, which made the Barn almost as Dusty as it was Outside of the Barn. Our Grandmother had to Clean the entire House, every Day, by Sweeping Up the Dust. The Dirt Floor could not be Mopped; but, it could be Swept. The Kitchen Table and Workbench were almost always Covered with a layer of Dust. The Dishes had to be Wiped Off, just to Eat; and, according to our Mother, the Foods almost always had Dust and Grit in them, which was enough to Wear Out their Teeths. In other Words, it was a Living Nightmare, for YEARS!) Meanwhile, the American Indians had their Way of Life RUINED by the Capitalists, who Shot the Buffaloes for the Sport of it, and left the Carcasses to ROT: beCause that is "the American Way of Practicing Capitalism," which is Related with "the American Dream," which is a very BAD Dream, in my Honest Opinion: beCause it has Produced X-amount of Criminals from the District of Criminals in Washington, all of the way Down to the Lowest Cockroaches in the City Dumps! (Our Dad spent several Years gathering up Buffalo Bones on his 4,480-acre Ranch in Montana, during the Great Depression, just to get a little extra Money for Buying Beans, Sugar, Coffee, and Flour. He Sold Truckloads of those Bones for making Bone Meal for Fertilizer for Gardens. The Bones had to be Cooked, Crushed, Ground, Dried, Packaged, and Shipped Eastward for Garden Stores. It has been Estimated that more than 60—100 Million American Bisons were Murdered in the Holy Names of "Progress" and "Capitalism." It would be like Killing all of the Wildebeests in Africa, just to get their Hides and Tongues. American Buffalo Hunters Salted and Smoked their Tongues, and sent them to Rich People in the East. Just one Smoked Beef Tongue is now on Sale for only 89 Dollars. The Buffalo Hunters got 10 Cents, and a couple of Dollars for a Buffalo Hide without any Scars nor Defects. They were often used to make Buffalo Robes or Cloaks, which were Popularized by Capitalist Advertisements.)

04-02 [_] O Selected King of **The Worldwide People's Revolution!®**, are those the Meanest Things that you can say about **"The Divided States of United Lies!" (The so-called "United State of North America" in Disguise!) By The Worldwide People's Revolution!®** Book 058? Why do you not become a TERRORIST and BOMB those SINators and CONgressmen? Indeed, why do you not Organize a Militia, and Take Over the Worthless Federal Government, and then take Down all of those Ugly Fences that Farmers and Ranchers have Installed to Murder Deers when they get Hung Up in them, while Attempting to Jump Over them, and thus Order those Farmers and Ranchers to Move into Cities of Confusion, where they can become Drug Dealers like George Washington, who was the Best American, who had more than a hundred Black and Brown Slaves to do his Dirty Work? †§‡§§ (See www.Amazon.com for: **"The BIG White OUTHOUSE on the Not-so-Biblical Capitol DUNGHILL!" (The Chief Sins of the Divided States of United Lies!) By The Worldwide People's Revolution!®** Book 023.}

04-03 [_] Well, I would much Prefer to bring all of them to COURT, and Prove them to be Chief Criminals, just for Promoting Capitalism, which Exploits the Earth for all that People can get from it, and then they Abandon it, just like they Abandoned the Indians, who are now Notorious Drunkards and Drug Addicts: beCause they have Lost their Faith, Hope, Trust, Love, Patience, Persistence, and Obedience, which are **"The Seven Basic Spiritual Building Blocks of LIFE!"** (See the Long List of Fascinating Literature at the Rear End of this Inspired Book.) Yes, it is Depressing, just to Study their Evil Situation, whereby they are STUCK in an "Eternal State of Extreme Poverty," even as the Ancient Animals were Stuck in Tar Pits, in California, and could not get themselves OUT. {See www.Amazon.com for: **"LIGHTNING STRIKES Versus Lightning Bugs!" (HOW you can Become Moderately RICH, without Telling any Lies nor Selling any Trash!)**, Book 074, plus: **"The GREAT Worldwide TELEVISED Court HEARING!" (That Great Meeting of the Most Intelligent and Well-Educated Minds!)**, Book 041 — at which Time the Leaders of all Nations will be Gathered Together for Discovering the Whole Truth about all Important Subjects, including the Evils of Capitalism. See also: **"The UGLY Scarred Dishonest Face of Poor Old Miserable UNCLE SAM!" (A Memorial Day Legacy!) By The Worldwide People's Revolution!®**, Book 054, which is a Companion Book of: **"Are Americans the Most STUPID People who ever Lived?" (HOW Working People can PROSPER and Live in PEACE Under the Rulership of a RIGHTEOUS KING!) By The Worldwide People's Revolution!®** Book 047.}

04-04 [_] So, O Selected King, if you had your Way, would you take Down all of the Fences, and let the Indians Return to their 1700's—1800's Lifestyles, and thus Live in TENTS? Or, would you Invite them to Build **"GLORIOUS Swanky Hotels Castles and Fortresses"** for themselves?

04-05 [_] Well, for Sure, I would Invite them to Help Build Fortresses for themselves: beCause of the Multitude of Good Reasons and Great Advantages for Doing it, and not just Talking about it. {See the above Link for: **"Mark Twain Races for the PRESIDENCY!" (The 2020 Presidential Candidates Desperately Need Some STRONG Undefeatable COMPETITION!)**, Book 33, plus: **"The Environmentalists' Paradise!" (HOW almost Everyone could be Living in a Beautiful Manmade Paradise!) By The Worldwide People's Revolution!®** Book 035.}

04-06 [_] O Selected King, how many Centuries would it Require for the Bisons to Repopulate themselves on the Great Plains, whereby they might Feed Americans all of the Buffalo Steaks that they might Want to EAT, seeing that there will be a BILLION of us within the next 100 or so Years? †§‡

(A List of the EVILS of CAPITALISM!)

04-07 [_] Well, if no one Killed them, until they got Old, and also left the Females to Live until they got Old, I would say that they would Repopulate the Great Plains within less than 100 Years; but, probably not to the Point that they were in 1800, where there were about 60 Million or more of them, as well as hundreds of Billions of Antelopes, Deers, Elks, Mooses, Beavers, and Countless Birds. Indeed, we cannot begin to Imagine what a Wonderland it was at that Time, before White People Moved in with their Capitalistic Evils, which begin with SELFISHNESS and GREED, and end with Divorce from God, Self-destruction, and Suicide! ‡

04-08 [_] So, O Selected King, it Appears like a very Bleak Future for Capitalism, which is Running on a Dead End Street, you might say, which will come to a HALT when we Run Out of Materials to EXPLOIT, huh?

04-09 [_] Yes, Capitalism Depends on Material Resources to Exploit — just like those Buffaloes; and therefore, when they Run Out of Gas, Oil, Coal, Trees, and Rivers of Water, they will be in BIG Trouble: beCause there will be little Energy for doing anything.

04-10 [_] It Sounds to me like the Perfect Setup for *the Great Tribulation and the Seven Last Great Plagues!*

— Chapter 05 —

Capitalism is Responsible for Pollutions, Worldwide

05-01 [_] There was a Time when the Detroit River was on FIRE: beCause of all of the Capitalist Pollution in it. However, that was not so Bad as Killing all of the Fishes in the Rivers, or at least Poisoning them with Mercury, Lead, Arsenic, Cadmium, and other "Heavy Metals," whereby few Rivers have Edible Fishes in them in **"The Divided States of United Lies,"** which Brags about being "the Greatest Nation in the World." Indeed, with such "Greatness," our Fame and Fortune is likely to reach into Heaven, where God will Write our Names in his Book of Life: beCause of being such Holy People. †§‡§§

05-02 [_] O Selected King, do you have any Idea how many Billions of Gallons of Toxic Wastes have been Dumped into our Rivers and Lakes — not to mention how we used those Rivers as Sewage Systems for 200 Years, before we Capitalists Realized that all such Water should be Drinkable, and GOOD to Drink?

05-03 [_] Well, I Seriously Doubt that anyone ever Bothered themselves to Measure just Exactly how much Toxic Poisons have been Dumped into Rivers and Lakes; but, we can be Sure that it was much more than was ever Reported. For Example, when my Brother Vern and I Lived on a Farm in Arkansas, there was a Semi-truck that passed by our Property, and Delivered a large Tank-load of Chemicals to a nearby Farm, not far from the Cossatot River, and ran it out into a Hole that was dug by a Bulldozer, which filled in the Hole, and Covered up the Outward Evidence, and some of the Horrible Smell, whereby we knew what they were up to. Moreover, we saw similar Trucks coming out of the Wildlife Preserve, where they had Obviously been Dumping Toxic Chemicals in the River, or on the Land: beCause there was no other Reason for them to be going in there. Furthermore, the EPA (Environmental Protection Agency) was not at all Interested in Checking it out: beCause of being Located more than 150 Miles away. Therefore, as far as we know, it went on for Years, and could still be going on, and perhaps once per Week or more. After all, the Wildlife Preserve is not Monitored by anyone; and the Naaber was likely Paid Off to keep his Mouth Shut. Therefore, if it went on over there, it probably goes on all over the Country — Thanks to Capitalism, which cannot Afford to Properly Dispose of all such Toxic Wastes, by making Congressmen Bathe in it, and then DRINK it, or Eat it in their Soups, since they Permit it! †§‡

05-04 [_] O Selected King, does ISIS (Israeli Secret Instigation Services) not Commit the same Kinds of Sins? Moreover, do all Nations not do the same Evil Things? Is not China the Worst?

05-05 [_] Well, I would say that China is most likely the Worst Polluters, just after the Divided States of United Lies: beCause they have taken up the Songs of the Capitalists, and have Determined to make a Living Hell for themselves, in the Name of Progress. Yes, they Learned HOW to Do it from US, and with less Regulations. After all, nothing should Stop the Goddess of "Progress," which is Determined to Transform the whole Earth into a Giant Toxic Trash Dump, like Long Island New York City, which is otherwise known as Satan's Dunghill, which could be Swept into the Atlantic Ocean by a Strong Hurricane and Rising Tides. †§‡

05-06 [_] O Selected King, do you suppose that we will have to go on a "Witch Hunt," just to Find all such Criminals, who would never Confess that they have Dumped Out BILLIONS of Gallons of Toxic Dung into the Forests, Rivers, Lakes, Seas and Oceans, all around the World?

05-07 [_] Well, when we Build those **"GLORIOUS Swanky Hotels Castles and Fortresses!" (Beautiful Planned City States for WISE Intelligent Well-Educated People with Common Sense and Good Understand!) By The Worldwide People's Revolution!®**, Book 019, we will likely have to make our own Brand New Topsoil: beCause of not being Able to Trust any Present Topsoil to be Healthy. After all, Billions of Tons of Toxic Dung have/has been Rained Down on the Lands all around the World: beCause of Spewing it into the Air — Thanks to Capitalism, which never Calculated the High Cost of it all. Therefore, the Children will have to Pay for the Environmental Sins of their Forefathers, one Way or another: beCause they have Inherited the Evil Deeds of the Synagogue of Satan, which is about to be put Out of Business; and thus the "Witches" will find themselves Living in Abandoned Cities of Confusion, eating Rats, Skunks, Snakes, and whatever they can Find.

05-08 [_] In other Words, O Selected King, they will not be Able to bring themselves around to Confess the Chief Capitalist Sins, huh?

05-09 [_] Well, that would be far too Humiliating for most Capitalists: beCause most of them do not even Want to Confess that there is some Connection between Cancers and Capitalist Abominations — such as those Cars, Vans, Pickups, Trucks, Buses, Motorcycles, Lawnmowers, Weed-eaters, Chainsaws, Motorboats, Mobile Homes, Fly Sprays, Solvents, Paints, and a whole List a Mile Long of Chemical Poisons, Household Cleaners, Herbicides, Pesticides, RAAD, LIISOL, BLEECH, and GMO Foods. Indeed, they Seek to Justify almost all of the Evils of Capitalism: beCause they are like the Silversmiths in *Acts 19,* who will Look rather Shameful during God's Judgment Day.

05-10 [_] So, O Selected King, it seems that Capitalism is a Special CULT of its own, which has Sucked In the Masses of People, who Actually Believe that it is GOOD, when it is Actually EVIL! Indeed, I Bet that you could List more than 500 Evils that can be Attributed to Capitalism, huh?

— Chapter 06 —

How many Evils can be Attributed to Capitalism?

06-01 [_] Well, since "Capitalism" Means: "The Love of Money in Action," almost all of the Evils in the World can be Attributed to it: beCause, *"the Love of Money"* is the Root Cause for almost all Evils, including those Hateful Wars, which are very Profitable for Weapons Manufacturers, Automobile Factories (which make very Expensive Vehicles for the Military, which must be of the Highest Qualities), Gas Companies (which Sell Gas for 400 Dollars per gallon in Afghanistan, for Example: because it is "Kosher Gas"), Airplane Manufacturers (which produce 250,000,000-dollar Jet Bombers, 100,000,000$ Helicopters, and 500,000$ Troop Transporters), Ammunition Factories (which Sell a 4$ Box of Ammunition for 400$ to the Tax Slaves, who do not Object: beCause only one Bullet in 10,000 or more ever Hit the Target), Drug Companies (which Sell hundreds of Billions of Dollars-worth of Drugs to the Government to "Treat" the Victims of Capitalist Wars), Medical Doctors (who get Paid 1,000$ per Hour for their Services to "Treat" the Victims of Lying Edomites), Hospitals (which Charge more Money for a Bed than the most Expensive Hotel in Town: beCause their Beds are Sanitary, being Sterilized by the People who Died on them, after being Overdosed on the WRong Prescription Drugs, which Kill upwards of 800- to 900-thousand "Patients" per Year in America, and no one says anything about it on the Evening Snooze Reports), Food Industries (which produce C-rations and whatever to Eat at the rate of 99$ per Meal, and it is hardly Edible), Clothes Makers and other Manufacturers, who make Uniforms, Boots, Helmets, Mess Kits, Gas Masks, Backpacks, Sleeping Bags, Tents, Mess Hall Equipment and Furniture, Bombs, Grenades, Missiles, Tools, and Coffins — all of which are Sold at 5 to 40 Times as much as the Actually Costs of them — Thanks to Capitalism. Indeed, even the Flower Shop Owners like those Gory Wars: beCause they are PROFITABLE! After all, who is more Worthy of Pretty Flowers around his Coffin, than some 18- or 19-year-old BABY Christian, who has never "red" the *Bible* so much as one Time from Cover to Cover, who is Unaware that Satan is in Charge of everything around here, and could Care Less if we ALL go to Hell? †§‡§§

06-02 [_] O Elected King, how Long will it Require for those Capitalists to Realize that there are other Wholesome Ways to Earn a Living, without going to War — such as Road Repairs? Indeed, the Dictionary Definition of *Capitalism* is this: *an economic and political system in which a country's trade and industry are controlled by private owners for profit, rather than by the state.* For Example, in the United States of America, the Governments Control the Construction of Highways and Bridges, which have nothing to do with Trade nor Industry — such Building Road Graders, Concrete Mixers and Bulldozers. And please do not Confuse us with the Facts. †§‡§§

06-03 [_] Well, the Edomite Bankers are the Holy Ones who stand to Gain the most Wealth from making Wars, Building Bridges and Highways: beCause all such Wars Cost TRILLIONS of Dollars, which must be Borrowed from those Friendly Bankers, and with Good Interest Payments:

The Nature of CAPITALISM!

beCause they are Worthy of hundreds of Billions of Dollars for doing almost NOTHING. Indeed, they might have to Write Checks, or perhaps only Sign a Name or 2, and thus Collect Billions of Dollars from the Tax Slaves, who can hardly Object: beCause, "if we do not Kill those Terrorists over there, they will be coming into our Living Rooms, over here!" In Fact, there is probably a Potential Terrorist Lurking behind every Tree and Bush in America, if not Up the Sleeves of Poor Pitiful Edomite Bankers. Likewise, when a Highway or Bridge is needed, the Poverty-stricken Government must Borrow the Money from those Friendly Banksters: because the Government never has Enough Money for doing anything: beCause its Treasury is always Purposefully EMPTY, in spite of the Federal Government Collecting more than 2 Trillion Dollars in Income Taxes, each Year: beCause the Revenue is Spent on Interest Payments to those Friendly Edomite Bankers, who Control the Money Supply, and thus Control the Government and the Stupid People who Support it by Election Deceptions, who have an Eternal HOPE that Congressman so-and-so will Fix it; but, he is just another Part of the Edomite Conspiracy against the Tax Slaves, who are Forever in Debt to the Edomites — Thanks to the Deceptions of Capitalism, whereby the Tax Slaves Vainly Imagine that they are in Control: beCause that is what the Definition of Capitalism Teaches them. Yes, the Tax Slaves are Free to get into Business for themselves, and "make" as much Money as they can, rather than "Earn" it by Honest Labor. However, in Reality, the Edomite Bankers are in Total Control of the Money Supplies and the Interest Money that might be Collected by them, no matter what the People nor Politicians might Vainly Imagine, who get farther and farther into Debt to those Edomites, who are Laughing all of the Way to their Banks. †§‡

06-04 [_] O Elected King of **The Worldwide People's Revolution!®**, I had a Capitalist Terrorist get into my own Pocket, you might say, and he Stole my Golden Eggs, and Disappeared!

06-05 [_] Chances are that he was very Hungry, in spite of Weighing 200 Pounds too much: beCause of Listening to Advertisements for Things to EAT. Indeed, we could make a List of those Evils to fill up a Book as big as the Bible: beCause the Motive for Selling all such "Junk Foods" is to Gain more Money, and 10 Times more Money than those Things are Worth, which is Capitalism. For Example, one of those 1$ Candy Bars might Cost all of 3 to 5 Cents to Produce it: beCause Machines do most of the Work, even as a Coke might Cost 2 to 3 Cents, except for the Aluminum Can, which might Cost all of 4 Cents, and can be Recycled for another Penny: beCause the "Soft Drinks" Companies Buy Things in HUGE Quantities, whereby they might get 100 pounds of White Refined Sugar for as little as 2$, which they Sell for 2,000$ in little Bottles: beCause there are about 10 Teaspoons of White Sugar in each Can of Coke. †§‡

06-06 [_] O Selected King, are you not Aware that you are Welcome to COMPETE with those Capitalists, and Sell your own "Soft Drinks" for a Profit? Indeed, anyone in the World is Welcome to set up his or her own Coke Factory, if he or she can Discover some Special Flavoring to Mix in with the Carbonated Water, which is Stored in HUGE Cisterns, whereby it goes Stagnant and Stale, and thus Tastes like it, if you just hold it in your Mouth and Taste of it, Carefully. In Fact the Flavor of Cocaine and Sugar is a Bit Overbearing; but, the Septic Tank Taste is still in the Coke, if you Taste for it, and can Recognize it. Moreover, Sensitive People can also Taste the Aluminum Can, and Recognize it as the Culprit that gives to Beer Drinkers a Metallic Breath, as if they were Eating Aluminum, which is most likely the Chief Cause for Alzheimer's Disease, and especially from Cooking Foods in Aluminum Kettles, as most Restaurants do, who are only Interested in PROFITS — NOT anyone's Good Health! †‡

(A List of the EVILS of CAPITALISM!)

06-07 [_] O Elected King, I would say that there must be no less than a Billion Evils that are Connected with Capitalism: beCause each Kind of Food and Drink is made the Way it is: beCause of GREED for more Money. For Example, there are many Kinds of Fruit Juice Drinks, which read: "100% Natural Juice" on the Label. However, if you read the Ingredients, you Discover that the First Ingredient is Recycled Sewage Water, which has been Recycled no less than 7 Times, after being Flushed Down Capitalist Drains into Sanitary Recycling Stations, which use Deadly Chemicals to "Purify" the Water, whereby it is called: "Purified Water" on the Label; and the Second Ingredient is White Refined Sugar, which is then Flavored with Orange Juice Concentrate, or some other "Natural" Juices, which have been Grown by: **"The LUSCIOUS All-Mineral ORGANIC Method of Gardening!" (HOW to Grow DELICIOUS Satisfying Foods for Potential Kingz and Kweenz in Beautiful Swanky PALACES!)**, Book 021, which Fruits were Sprayed with Deadly Poisons no less than 16 Times per Growing Season by Holy Angels, who are Paid 16 Cents per Hour for their Labors, Spraying and Picking Fruits for the Apostles, who have now Contracted Various Kinds of Glorious Cancers! And I am not being Sarcastic. †§‡§§

06-08 [_] O Elected King, I have Noticed all of my Life that the FRONT Side or Street Side of most Businesses in Town are Looking pretty Good; but, if you go around to the BACKSIDES of all such Businesses, they usually Look pretty DUMPY, as if nobody Cared HOW the Backsides Look, which is also True of their Painted Houses, which often have Rotting Roofs on the Backsides, or Dilapidated Porches, or Bathrooms that need several thousand dollars-worth of Repairs: beCause of being Designed by Satan and Sons, Incorporated, to begin with. After all, if their Walls were made of Solid Concrete, and Tiled with Polished Marble, or Beautiful Ceramic Tiles, they would not Need Painting. ‡ (See the Photo on Page 3, which shows Part of a 10,000-gallon Cistern that I built with my own Hands during 6 Months for our Retirement Home. Strangely enough, none of the Tiles have Fallen Off — not even on the Ceiling of it! I Wonder WHY? The Ceiling is 100% Solid Homemade Concrete, made with Clean Sand and Gravel. Vern and I Washed 50 Dump Truckloads of Gravel by Hand for our Retirement Home, in Order to Remove no less than 50 Barrels of MUD: beCause Cement does not Stick very Well to Mud; and yet most Concrete is made with the Mud in it, in Mexico: beCause that Assures the American Cement Company of Selling more Cement for Highways and Houses that must be Replaced: beCause of Deteriorating Concrete. Indeed, it might Cost all of 2 or 3 Dollars to Wash the Gravel Properly for 7 Cubic Meters of Concrete; but, why bother with it, seeing that it is much more Profitable to leave the Mud in the Gravel, whereby the Work Slave who Buys the Concrete can be Happy for it: beCause he cannot See the Mud, and is not Aware of what it is Doing to his Concrete — that is, until an Earthquake comes along and Ruins it: beCause it Crumbles? †§‡§§) {See: **"What is WRong with those CRAZY Christians?" (A Self-Examination of the Heart of the Body of Good Government!) By The Worldwide People's Revolution!®**, Book 076, which shows many Photographs with Explanations of our Retirement Home Construction Project. We Moved more than 66 Million Pounds by Hand to Build it!}

06-09 [_] Well, the Reason most American Walls are not made of Solid Concrete, is beCause all such Houses must be Insulated with Fiberglass, Styrofoam, or some other Abomination, which is Highly Toxic when it BURNS: beCause Capitalism does not give a Damn about the Air, Water, Land, People, Animals, Trees, Gardens, nor anything else. Indeed, all Houses could have Solid Stone Walls that are 10 Feet THICK, whereby no Insulation, Heating, nor Cooling Bills are Needed! Indeed, it is Actually much less Expensive in the Long Run, whereby you can Pay for such a Good Wall with just a few Years of NOT Paying for Insurance, Heating, Cooling, Painting, and Needless Repair Bills — not to Mention those Needless Property Taxes. Moreover, I am talking about a Roof that is a Minimum of 10 Feet THICK, whereby a Garden is on every Roof: so that no Space is Wasted. Indeed, they are called Beautiful Stone Dome Home Complexes, which are Designed for Eternal Employment, at HOME, or near Home! {See www.Amazon.com for: **"The Right Design for Living!" (A List of Great Advantages for Building Beautiful Planned City States!)**, which has many Drawings in it for you to Study, along with Explanations.}

06-10 [_] So, O Elected King of **The Worldwide People's Revolution!®**, would such a House have WINDOWS in it? I cannot Imagine Living in a House without Windows to Open for Fresh Air and Sunlight.

06-11 [_] Well, each Stone Dome would have to have a Skylight / Vent in the Ceiling, with a Closable Door on Top of the Skylight, which is Controlled by a Cable and Lever within the Dome, whereby you could Open the Window on Top of the Skylight, and thus Vent the Room as much as you might like; but, not let Out all of the Heat during Winter Months, nor let IN too much Heat during Hot Summer Days.

06-12 [_] So, O Selected King, HOW would we keep the Horrible HUMIDITY Out of such a House, seeing that it would be Cool and Comfortable during those Hot Summer Months — except for that Humidity?

06-13 [_] Well, each Swanky Stone Dome Home Complex needs a large ICE House under it, whereby all of that Humidity is SUCKED OUT of the House: beCause of being Attracted to the ICE below it, which Moisture passes through Convenient Trap Doors in the Floors, which Regulates the Humidity, for FREE, you might say: beCause of the Ice House, which is made Possible by Building the whole City in TERRACES, whereby your Garden is on the Roof of the Family who Lives BELOW you in the next Terrace. Indeed, you will not have to Climb Steps nor take an Elevator to get to your own Garden: beCause it is Conveniently Located Directly in Front of your House, and NOT in any so-called "Backyard": beCause there are NO Backyards. However, your Personal Ice House is UNDER the Stone Dome Home Complex in the Terrace ABOVE you: so that your Ice House is also on the same Level or Floor as your own House, which is Accessible by Means of an Underground Tunnel, which is no less than 6 feet Wide, just in case you have to Haul Ice or something else through that Tunnel in a Cart with 2 large Wheels, like a Heavy-duty 26-inch Bicycle Wheel with Solid Spokes, which Carts are Designed to Endure the Test of Time, being made mostly of Aluminum with Welded Joints, having Strong 1-inch Hardened Stainless Steel Axles: so that all such Carts may Carry a Load of 400 or more Pounds throughout the Fortress, which will have large Spacious Tunnels for Public Transportation, as well as large Spacious Elevators, and Slow-moving Trains with Cars that are 20 feet Wide and 100 feet Long, which are Designed for Transporting those "Grocery Carts," and even Quadrupeds, Bicycles, Furniture, and whatever: beCause no other Vehicles will be Needed. However, if someone is in a Hurry, he or she may get on a Speedy Electric Train in another Tunnel, and also go from a Central Station Directly to another Swanky Fortress, by Means of Underground Trains, and without the Risks of Terrorists Attacking: beCause no Terrorists will be Permitted within any such Planned Cities, who will be Discovered when they are Children, and thus be Corrected or BANISHED.

06-14 [_] So, O Elected King, suppose there is not Sufficient Cold Weather to make enough Ice for those Ice Houses — what shall we Do for Ice?

(A List of the EVILS of CAPITALISM!)

06-15 [_] Well, it could be that Ice will have to be Transported from wherever there is Enough Cold Weather to Produce it, which is still much Cheaper than running Freezers to make Ice: beCause Ice Trains can also Run Underground on Level Ground from the Mountains: beCause of using Elevators for each Boxcar. Indeed, a Boxcar can be Filled with Ice-water just Deep enough to Freeze Solid, and then more Ice-water can be Added to it the next Night, at the Top of some Mountain, above the Railroad Tracks, where the Boxcars are Resting and Freezing the Ice, until the Insulated Boxcar is FULL of Ice; and then it is let Down the Elevator, which is Perfectly Balanced on it Cables with Appropriate Weights in the Elevator, so that no Energy is Wasted in Transporting the Boxcar to the Railway: beCause the Weights are made of ICE, which is then Moved into Empty Boxcars, before the Elevator is Raised for the next Boxcar with Ice, which may Require a Week or more to have a Solid Block of Ice in that Boxcar, which is then run Directly into an Ice House from a Special Railway Line that passes by each Stone Dome Home Complex from Underground, which is only Used once per Year, during the Winter Months, whereby each Stone Dome Home Complex is Supplied with a Year or more of ICE, which is Used Wisely for Walk-in Coolers, Freezers, Swanky Refrigerators, and so on, which will make it Possible to Live Comfortably in any HOT Humid Place on the Earth! Indeed, it may be very Humid OUTSIDE; but, not within the Houses. Another Option is to make an Ice Train that runs into an Ice Tunnel behind a Long Row of Stone Dome Home Complexes on one Terrace, which is Accessed from each House by a Short Tunnel. The Ice Train would come once every 10 Years or so with a New Load of Ice. After all, a Chunk of Ice that is about 100 feet long and 20 feet wide and 10 feet thick is not going to Melt very Quickly in a Well-Insulated Swanky Ice House at 40 °F below Zero. ‡

06-16 [_] So, O Elected King, that is something that could only be Accomplished by **"Seven Great Armies of Working Soldiers!" (HOW to Provide a Way for Everyone to WORK: so as to Eliminate Poverty, Crimes, Drug Abuses, Prisons, and Unnecessary Taxes!)**, Book 015, huh?

06-17 [_] Indeed, it would be very Impractical for an Independent Jackass to Move Ice from Wisconsin or North Dakota to Houston, Texas, for Example, by Means of a Garden Cart; and it would be Terribly Expensive to Move 40 Tons of Ice by Means of Trucks, when Compared with a Swanky Electric Train on a Level Underground Track, which Train might be 100 Miles Long. ‡

06-18 [_] So, O Master Architect, how many Centuries would be Required for Building all such Railroads? Is it not also very Expensive to make Underground Railways for Boxcars that are 20 feet in Diameter and 100 feet Long and 10 feet High?

06-19 [_] Well, if we Plan it Correctly, there will only be a Need for ONE such Railroad from Canada to Mexico, which can Branch Out, here and there, in Order to Service all Points East and West on the Great Plains, where we can also Build 2 or 3 Giant Swanky Fortresses for nearly all Americans and Mexicans: beCause, just one such City will be able to Contain no less than 100,000,000 People! For Example, there are about 268,580 square Miles in Texas, alone, which Means that there are no less than 128,000,000 Acres in Texas — not Counting Lakes nor Rivers, which Means that each Family could have a one-Acre Garden in front of their House, as well as a one-Acre Stone Dome Home Complex with Domes and Tunnels, while having Underground Tunnels for many Kinds of Quiet Electric Trains. Indeed, it is an Architect's Dream Project to Design, Properly, which will Require the Best Architects in the World, along with the Best Drawing Programs on Computers. ‡

06-20 [_] So, O Elected King, would each Household have a Barrel-vault Ice House that is Big Enough to Contain a Boxcar that is 100 feet Long and 20 feet Wide?

06-21 [_] Yes, the Train Track would be Inside of one Long Ice House, which would be a Barrel-vault Tunnel 40 feet Wide and 20 feet Tall, and made Especially for the Ice Train, which would let off a Boxcar directly behind each Stone Dome Home Complex, whereby each Family in each Great Terrace would have their own HUGE Block of ICE, which would Endure for no less than 4 or 5 Years; but, most likely for 10 Years or more. Therefore, if there is Freezing Weather in Canada at least once every 4 or 5 Years, then it will be Possible to make ICE, and LOTS of it: beCause much of Canada is FRESH WATER, which can be Pumped into those Special Boxcars, which have Sloping Sides: so that no Damage can be done to the Boxcars by the Thawing Ice, which can be Frozen in Layers, as it is Needed, and then Transported all of the Way to Panama on Ice Trains, where the Melted Ice can be Used Wisely for Watering Gardens, Vineyards and Orchards, after Cooling Off and Dehumidifying the Houses, wherever it is Needed in Yucatan, for Example, which is a Vast Unpopulated Territory, which has a Perfect Climate for Growing Mangos, Coconuts, Papayas, and many Kinds of Tropical Fruits, including Dates, Figs, and Cherimoyas, which are really GOOD Sweet Fruits to Eat: beCause they do not Ruin your Teeth like Acid Fruits. ‡

06-22 [_] So, O Elected King of **The Worldwide People's Revolution!**®, is it Fair to say that you have LOST your Riit Miind? Would a whole Third of Americans Willing Choose to Live in the Hateful State of TEXAS, which has Extremes in the Weather, which can Drop Down to 10 below Zero Degrees Fahrenheit from 70 °F during just ONE Night!?

06-23 [_] Well, that is a very Good Reason to Want to Live in Yucatan, where the Temperatures are Moderated by the Gulf of Mexico. After all, that is where the Ancient Mayan Indians built the Great Pyramids, and many Stone Buildings — such as those in Uxmal (Qshmawl), Palenque (Paalenkaa), and Chichen Itza (Cheechen Eetsu), which are only Rivaled by the Great Pyramids in Egypt, which are far Outnumbered in Mexico, which has about 3,000 Pyramids!

06-24 [_] So, O Elected King of **"The New RIGHTEOUS One-World Government,"** if we got Together with those Mexicans, and Humbled ourselves, and Built a Great Swanky Fortress in Yucatan, would it not Interfere with those Ancient Monuments?

06-25 [_] Well, actually, the Fortress could be Designed to Incorporate the Pyramids within it: so as to take Better Care of them, and make them more Available for Visitors, who might Decide to Live there, just to Explore those Pyramids, and Study them. After all, there are still lots of Mysteries involved in their Constructions. (See *Wikipedia* for more Details.)

06-26 [_] So, O Selected King of the Ignorant Fools, suppose all of the People in the Whole World Decide that they Want to Live in Yucatan with its Fair Weather at a half-mile Up in the Sky in a Swanky Fortress — how will they be Accommodated? Moreover, might that Cause Yucatan to Break Off of Mexico, and Fall into the Gulf of Mexico?

06-27 [_] Well, there are many Places in this World of Wonders, which would be Ideal for Living at the Correct Elevation, which can be made Possible by those Great Terraces, even in the HOT Humid Jungle of Brazil, which just Requires more Elevation. But, the Brazil Nut Trees might not Like it, along with many other Kinds of Tropical Trees and Plants. Therefore, it is probably Better to leave Brazilian Jungles alone, and let them be National Parks for Monkeys and many other Wild Animals, having only Small Swanky Fortresses for Visitors, who Want to come to Watch the Monkeys and other Animals Play among the Trees.

06-28 [_] So, O Elected King, would we Tear Down the Mountains in Alaska, just to Raise Up those Terraces in Hot Places like Africa, which has few Mountains?

06-29 [_] Well, I would say that that would be much Better than Americans Wasting a Trillion Gallons of Gas at Capitalist Stop Lights, each Year. What do you Think?

06-30 [_] O Selected King, you do not Want to HEAR what I might Think about your Pessimistic Plan to Save the World by doing Away with our Beloved Cars, Vans, Pickups, Trucks, Buses, Motorboats, Mobile Homes, Lawnmowers, Weed-eaters, Chainsaws, and our most Beloved Airplanes. After all, we would be Returning to the 16th Century! Indeed, the American Bisons would be Roaming on the Great Plains with the Deers and Antelopes, and nobody would even Leave a Swanky Fortress, if we all got Settled Down in them, except to go Visit other **"GLORIOUS Swanky Hotels Castles and Fortresses!" (Beautiful Planned City States for WISE Intelligent Well-Educated People with Common Sense and Good Understanding!) By The Worldwide People's Revolution!® Book 019.** Indeed, **"The LUSCIOUS All-Mineral Organic Method of Gardening"** would have everyone Addicted to all of those DELICIOUS Fruits and Vegetables, whose Flavors and Fragrances would be no less than 10 Times as Good as our Present Insipid Fruits and Vegetables. Therefore, WHY would anyone Want to Live in some Low-class City of Confusion, where Criminals are Roaming about on the Streets, where Terrorists are Lurking behind every Bush and Tree, where one cannot Safely go Shopping, where the Children are using Illegal Drugs, and no one knows HOW to Stop it — except for YOU, O Master Magician? †§‡ (See www.Amazon.com for the above Books, and many more.)

{FOOTNOTE: I bought 2 Tamales this morning for my Brother, and the "Businesswoman" who made them said that they had lots of Chicken and Cheese in them; but, Vern did not Discover either one in the Tamales, which were at least 98% Horse Corn with some Chili Flavoring: beCause it is Extremely Difficult for a True Capitalist to be Perfectly Honest. Indeed, you might Think that People would not do Business with her: beCause of being Offended by her Lies; but, when there are so many Potential Customers, she can Afford to be Dishonest, and even Charge more than Good Tamales would Cost with lots of Chicken: beCause that is the Advantage of Telling Lies. She Charged 8 Pesos for just one Tamale. Another Tamale Lady, who Works farther away by a couple of Miles or more, Sells really Good Tamales with the Correct Amount of Chicken and Cheese and Chili Spices for only 5 Pesos, each, whereby a Customer can get as many as 20 Tamales for only 100 Pesos, or about 5 Dollars, which would be only enough Money to Buy 2 or 3 Tamales in **"The Divided States of United Lies!" (The so-called "United States of North America" in Disguise!) Book 058.** In other Words, a little Money goes a long ways in Mexico, which Actually has a Higher Standard of Living: beCause of not having so many Bills to Pay. For Example, no one Buys Insurance for their Concrete Houses: beCause Fire does not Hurt Concrete very much. I have yet to Hear of a Mexican House Burning Down. It has likely never Happened. But, if it did Happen, we could Blame it on American Capitalist Influences: beCause of Capitalists Wandering across the Border from the Divided States of United Lies, while Dragging their Capitalist Deceptions along behind them! For Example, Home Depot sells Imitation Wood Paneling for Mexicans to put on their Walls and Floors, whereby their Houses are filled with the Toxic Odors of Plastic Paneling, which gives to them Headaches, which Drives them to the Pharmacy to Buy Pain-killing Pills, which Causes other Ailments, which Drives them to the Medical Doctors, who Prescribe other Expensive Pills, whereby they finally end up in an American Capitalist HELL HOLE! And that is the Nature of CAPITALISM!}

— Chapter 07 —

A Multitude of Little Capitalist Sins

07-01 [_] Perhaps you have gone Shopping for Tools of some Kind, without Realizing that there is a Great Deal of DIFFERENCE Between the "Holy" and the "Unholy," as the *Bible* puts it. Indeed, some Tools are little Better than TRASH, and can Break or easily be Damaged the very first Time that you Use them. For Example, I had 10 Acres of Grass and Weeds to Mow Off on our Farm, Years ago, and I Decided to Experiment with Lawnmowers, since I had nothing Better to Do at that Time for Exercise: beCause of not having Enough Money for Building anything; but, I did have Enough Money for Capitalist Experimentations — such as Mulching the Sweet Corn in the Garden with Grass Clippings, and TONS of them. Yes, it was WORK, even with a Partially Self-propelled "Push-and-Pull" Lawnmower, which went Forward, at least some of the Time; but, not Backwards, which meant that I had to Pull it Backwards in many Situations, which made it a Sweaty Job at 90 to 110 °F in Arkansas, during the Summertime, and during 7 Years of that Capitalist Madness, whereby I went through no less than 7 Lawnmowers, including 2 Troy-bilt Lawnmowers, and 2 DR Field Brush Mowers, and one Rechargeable ElecTRICK Lawnmower, and a Weed Trimmer, which was Self-propelled, made by Troy-bilt, which had Guarantees on their Equipment.

07-02 [_] For Example, the Troy-bilt Lawnmower with a Bag had a One-year Warranty, which I took full Advantage of, and it Broke Down the very First Day that I ran it. So, we took it back to *John Deer*, for Repairs: because they were Selling them, and for a Hefty Profit; and 2 Months later they Informed me that the Correct Part was no longer Available: beCause Troy-bilt had gone Out of Business. Nevertheless, they Promised to Fix it by one Means or another, whereby I got it back on the Farm within another Month, and then, within another Week, it Broke Down again! So, we took it back, 50 Miles to Texarkana, for Repairs, and got it back 6 Months later, which was Long Past the Season when we Needed it. So, we got Frustrated, and thus got another Lawnmower — Thinking that perhaps between the 2 of them, the Capitalists might be Able to keep them Operating! Yes, it was a Good Self-deception: beCause none of those Lawnmowers were Designed for the Job of Lawn-mowing in Arkansas, which does have some fairly Tough Weeds to Mow Off. However, we were Assured by the Salesman that those Weeds would be no Problem, if we just took our Time, and Mowed with Patience, which I did: beCause Vern Refused to Run it: beCause of the STINK and NOISE that was put out by it. (He much Preferred the Periodical Farts of Mules.) Indeed, before that Time, we had 3 Mules to use; but, one Day the County Vet showed up to Test them for some Highly Contagious Disease among Horses, whereby the 2 Best Mules Tested POSITIVE, which Meant that they had to be Shipped Off to some Slaughterhouse for Dog Food at ONE-TENTH of their Original Price that Vern had Paid for them! And the other one we Hauled all of the way to Kentucky, to be Sold to some Mennonites, which Covered the Cost of the Propane Gas for the Pickup, and nothing more. Meanwhile, that Mule was Crying all of the Way over there, being Heartbroken for being Separated from the other Mules, who were also Crying with Big Tears when we left the Farm with them, to which they were Bonded for 10 Years, or more, and not only to the Farm; but, to us and Vern's 6 Children, also, which was Heartbreaking: beCause they were Pets of the most Valuable Kind: beCause of all of the Difficult Work that they could do, and did Do without any Complaints, Protests, Riots, Strikes, nor Sit Downs on the Jobs.

(A List of the EVILS of CAPITALISM!)

07-03 [_] So, O Selected King, were those Mules never Sick? Could they do a Full Day's Work on your 7 Acres of Gardens?

07-04 [_] Absolutely, they were Strong Healthy Mules, who were just "Carriers" of the Horse Disease, which did not Effect them at all. Nevertheless, being in a "free" Country, we were Ordered to get Rid of them. Therefore, who were we to be Bucking up against the County "Authorities"?

07-05 [_] O Selected King, if it had been ME, I would have Lost my Temper, and Filled that Veterinarian with some 00 (double ought) Buckshot from my Shotgun, which is used for Bear Hunting, which would have left a Hole in his Loins no less than 8 inches in diameter! Indeed, I would not have even Warned him to Stay Away from my Farm. After all, there was Obviously nothing WRong with those Mules, who were not in any Contact with any Horses, since your Farm was Bordered by a Road on 2 Sides, and Fragrant Chicken Houses and Hog Sheds on the other 2 Sides. Therefore, no other Horses could have Contacted them. †§‡

07-06 [_] Well, all of that is True, my Friend. However, neither one of us had any Longing Desire to Waste the Remainder of our Lives in some All-American Prison, when it was so much easier to just Submit to our Cruel Capitalist Masters, who seemed to be Determined to get Rid of the Last Vestiges of Mule Drivers in the World — at least in our known World.

07-07 [_] So, O Elected King, did the 2 Lawnmowers Work Well for you after that, after Obeying the Commandment of God to LOVE and OBEY whatever Government Authorities are Set Up by God over you, who Determines WHO the Leaders of all Nations will be?‡ (See *Romans 13, KJV.*)

07-08 [_] No. In Fact, we made no less than 50 Trips for 50 Miles, one Way, just to Honor that Guarantee on the Second Lawnmower, which Broke Down about every other Day! Therefore, I at least got a Break between Mowings, which usually Required 2 to 3 Days to get it "Fixed," which meant that we had to Waste some more Gas: beCause it was the nearest White Lawnmower Repair Shop around. Indeed, it was Cheaper than Buying a New Self-propelled Sneers and Rowbuck Lawnmower for 499$, plus Tax: because it was on Sale for only 400$, which ended up Costing 4,500$! After all, Propane was only 50 Cents per Gallon at that Time, and therefore we could fill up our "100-gallon Tank" on the 1972 International Pickup Truck for only 40$: beCause it did not Actually HOLD 100 Gallons: beCause that is another Trick of Capitalists, who tell little Lies. Nevertheless, we did fill up with Propane one Time, in Hazard, Kentucky, and Drove all of the Way to Texarkana on that one Tank of Gas, and could have most likely made it all of the Way Home; but, then we would not have had enough Gas to get back to Town for more of it — Thanks to Capitalism. In Fact, we ran Out of Gas, one Time, and had to Sleep in the Pickup, until the next Morning, when a Delivery Truck brought a Load to us for a 10$ Service Charge, which would now Cost no less than 100$ — Thanks to Inflationary Capitalism. †

07-09 [_] So, O Selected King, did you not get Tired of Lawn-mowering after 7 Years of that Self-inflicted Torment?

07-10 [_] Well, I was Tired of it after just one Day; but, I Wanted to get that Sweet Corn MULCHED with Grass Clippings, which I did the next Year, when we got a DR Field and Brush Mower and a Rake, whereby we gathered up Tons of Clippings, and Carefully Placed them around the Plants in our one-acre Garden on Top of the Hill, which was Working quite Well, until a Family of Raccoons just Happened to Discover them a Day or 3 before they were Ready to Harvest, who Kindly went down each Row, and Pulled Down each Cob, and Tasted of it, only to Discover that it was not quite Ready to Eat, whereupon I got all of 3 Cobs of Corn to Eat for 3 Months of Hard Work, and Vern got 5 Cobs. And that is the Capitalist Method at its Best! {See: **"Orgimmick Gardening at its Best!" (HOW to Grow Delicious Satisfying Foods without a 10-Million-Dollar Investment!) By The Worldwide People's Revolution!®** Book 079.}

07-11 [_] So, O Selected Fool of **The Worldwide People's Revolution!®**, did that not Discourage you and Vern from doing any more Organic Gardening? Why did you not put up a Good Fence around that Corn Patch, first?

07-12 [_] Well, we Thought of it afterwards; but, it was the First Time that those Raccoons got that Bold. Perhaps the Mules and Goats had Spooked them away at other Times. Who knows? At any rate, it Inspired us to Build a Special Garden, just for Sweet Corn, which was also Effective for keeping the Crows Out of the Corn: because that Garden has 2 Concrete Walls around it, whereby Dogs can Patrol the Area, if need be. Then we also Installed High Fences on those Concrete Walls, whereby only the most Bold Raccoon would Dare get himself in there: beCause the Concrete was SLICK, like Polished Marble: beCause we used Plastic Sheeting Inside of the Concrete Forms, which left the Concrete Smooth when it was Removed. Therefore, no Raccoons ever got into that Corn Patch. Then we put Steel Posts every 4 feet, all around the Garden, in the Concrete Walls: so as to be able to Install Fishing Lines across the Garden in both Directions, whereby Mr. Crow could not figure out HOW to Fly between those Lines: beCause, when he Attempted to do it, his Wings would get Hung Up in the Lines, if his Neck did not get Broken. Therefore, one Crow must have told all of the other Crows to Stir Clear of that Corn Patch: beCause we never Lost so much as one Cob to the Crows, nor to anything else, except for the Naaberz, who Discovered it, whereby we Installed 4,000-dollars-worth of Steel Gates with Locks for Protection, which still Failed to Keep Out the Tax Masters, who Naturally Calculated that those Walls and Gates were Taxable. In Fact, if you are so Foolish as to put Stone or Concrete Walls around all of your Property, you can Pay thousands of dollars per Year for that "Sin," which can Cause you to Lose the entire Farm! For Example, one of our Distant Naaberz was Taxed 15,000$ per Year for a Farm with less than 10,000$ Income: beCause of his Capitalist "Sins." Therefore, you have to Watch in Front of your Back, as well as Behind it. †

07-13 [_] So, O Selected King, would a Swanky Fortress not have the same Raccoon Problem?

07-14 [_] Well, rather than each Person Building his or her Private Fortress Walls around his or her Private Property, there could be just 2 Concentric Walls around the entire Fortress, with MOATS around them, whereby even the Tax Masters could be Kept Out, which would also Save thousands of Miles of Needless Walls, which would be like putting a Wall around a Checkerboard, as opposed to putting a Wall around each Square on the Checkerboard. In other Words, if each Square on the Checkerboard were 10 Acres, and the whole Checkerboard were one Square Mile, having 64 Farms, each Farm would Require a Wall around it, whereby just 8 Farms would have an equal number of Linear Feet of Walls as the entire Square Mile; or, 8 Times as many Walls as would be Needed to keep out the Raccoons, Snakes, Rats, Mice, Opossums, Skunks, and whatever might get in. Therefore, if there are that many Walls on just one Square Mile of Land, try to Imagine how many Walls would be Needed for 328,000,000 Acres of Land, scattered out all over the UNITED States of Confusion? But, to make it even Worse, Imagine 300,000,000 Little

(A List of the EVILS of CAPITALISM!)

Gardens that are barely large enough to Grow a dozen Cabbages, and no Space for Fruit nor Nut Trees, much less Walk-in Coolers for Storing all such Fruits, Nuts and Vegetables, which not one Person in a Million has — Thanks to Capitalism! Indeed, almost no one could Afford such Coolers, Ice Houses, Freezers, and SAFE Stone Dome Homes, which are Terrorist-proof and School Shootings-proof and Mass-Murdering-proof. (Remember Lost Wages, Nevada, whereby a Mass-Murderer Killed 58 People, and Wounded hundreds in just Minutes!)

07-15 [_] So, O Selected King, are you Suggesting that every American NEEDS a Garden and Orchard, just to be Healthy, Wealthy, and WISE?

07-16 [_] Well, if they Sincerely Want to Prosper as God Intended, they will have to Move Over to the Garden of Eden Lifestyle, which is much more Simple and Beautiful in all Ways. After all, who has any Longing Desire to go to Hell for the Sake of being Able to Drive a Car around, and Boast about being FREE, when almost all Americans are Insurance Slaves, Interest Slaves, Tax Slaves, and Work Slaves, which can be Proven in a Courtroom?

07-17 [_] So, O Selected King, what are some of the other little Sins of Capitalism?

07-18 [_] Well, speaking of those Capitalist Tools, I Experimented with Maytag Washing Machines, which Costed 1,100$ each: beCause the first one Broke Down within a Month or so; and therefore, I took it for Repairs, and got it back 3 Months later. Meanwhile, needing a Washing Machine Daily on the Farm: because of Sweaty Clothes, I decided to get another 1,100$ Maytag Washing Machine for a "Spare Tire," you might say, along with a Service Agreement for 250$ per Year, whereby it got Repaired no less than 8 Times within 2 Years, along with the first Machine: beCause there was some Defective Capitalist's Part in the Electronic System that was not Designed Correctly, which Costed Maytag about 300$ per Pop, whereby they Lost any Profits on the Machines, and finally Moved to Mexico, if I heard it Correctly. In other Words, I Paid 250 Dollars for the Service Agreement, while Maytag Paid 2,400 Dollars for their Repairs. What a Good Deal for the Capitalists, huh? †‡

07-19 [_] So, O Selected King, it seems that you have a lot of Bad Luck with Capitalist Machines, huh?

07-20 [_] Well, if you Recall your History Lessons, Mark Twain also had similar Problems with all such Machines, and Lost tens of thousands of Dollars on Bad Investments, while Failing to Invest in Bell Telephone, which could have made him very Rich. However, unlike him, I have never Invested a Dime in any such Industries: beCause of Realizing what Scams they are, and what Great False Riches are Promised by Capitalists. Yes, it is the Nature of Capitalism, which makes a few Rich Hogs Richer with the False Riches, while the Masses of People must go on Suffering for their Unbelief in my Inspired Words of Provable Truths: beCause they are Basically just IDIOTS, who have been made into Independent Capitalist Idiots by the Public School of Ignorant Fools and the Greatly Worshiped Television, which Advertises Endless Capitalist Trash for Sale, which no one ever Needed for True Prosperity, which Requires a GOOD Reliable Supply of Fresh Pure Living Water, which no one on the Earth has, as far as I know. Indeed, if you know of such a Person, please let me know WHO and WHERE he or she Lives: beCause I have yet to Discover such a Person, even though there is a Natural Living Spring of Water coming down from the German Mountains in Southern Bavaria, near to the Neuschwanstein Castle — that is, the New

Beautiful Swan Castles in Southern Germany, which you can Learn about in *Wikipedia*. The Spring is not on Private Property; but, you are Welcome to Drink all of the Living Water that you might Want, which will make you Feel like a New Person, all over: beCause it is really GOOD Living Water. Meanwhile, check out the Photos in *Wikipedia* for that Beautiful Castle.

— Chapter 08 —

Capitalists have Ruined the Water Supply

08-01 [_] Acid Rains fall on the Land, bringing down Mercury, Lead, Arsenic, Cadmium, Aluminum, and whatever has been Spewed into the Air by Industries, Factories, Vehicles, Airplanes and whatever — Thanks to Capitalism. It is Estimated that there are presently a Trillion Tons of all such Capitalist Dung in our Atmosphere, which would Require a hundred Years or more just Clear Away, even if we now Totally Stopped putting any more of it up there! However, to make Matters Worse, the Wicked Federal Government is Permitting, or even Orchestrating, what are known as Chemtrails or Chemical Trails in the Sky, whereby millions of tons of Aluminum are Deliberately Spewed into the Atmosphere, which has been Proven by Scientists who have Studied Lakes and Lands before and after the Sprayings. You might have also Noticed such Chemtrails, which you might Believe are only Condensation Trails from Jet Airplanes. However, those "Contrails" quickly Disperse in the Air, while "Chemtrails" can hang around all Day. Notice that Wikipedia refers to such Scientists as: Chemtrail Conspiracy Theorists — as if it were not Proven to be True. You can find much Evidence on YouTube Videos for Proof. Most People are not Old enough to Remember when the Skies were Clear, without any Trails of anything in the Sky. However, I was Born and Raised in the Wide-open Spaces of Montana, which is now Nicknamed "the Big Sky Country": because of a Big Clear Sky, since very few Airplanes are in the Sky over Montana and Canada, which have some of the Best Views in the World. However, with Tourism in the millions of People per Year, the Air in Montana is not what it used to be; but, the Pollution is still a little "Thinner" than it is in Populated Places throughout the World, which is so "Thick" in Beijing, China, most of the Time, that one cannot see anything clearly more than one City Block from where one is standing, while in Montana, one might see Clearly for 200 Miles on a Clear Day, which is also True of Canada, Siberia, Africa, Parts of South America, and even Western China.

08-02 [_] So, O Selected King, if a Person is not Choking to Death on the Bad Air, or Caused to Faint from Drinking a single Glass of Poisonous Water, such a Person just Naturally pays little Attention to the Environmental Conditions, huh?

08-03 [_] Well, many People Choose to Work in very Polluted Conditions — such as those of Welders, who Breathe Bad Air for most of their Working Hours, while also Smoking Cigarettes; and then they Wonder WHY they Contract Lung Cancers and other Ailments? So, it is Obvious that People can Tolerate a High Level of Pollution without Dropping Over Dead: beCause God Designed us that Way. In Fact, it used to be that American Indians built little Fires right inside of their Teepees / Tents, and thus Breathed Wood Smoke for most of the Winter, while many Houses

(A List of the EVILS of CAPITALISM!)

in Europe had no Chimneys for thousands of Years: beCause they did similar Things. In Fact, London was so Full of Toxic Smoke at one Time from Burning Coal in Stoves, that People were Dropping Dead on the Streets, and then it crossed the Minds of Government Officials that it was Necessary to Do something about it; but, it never crossed their Weak Minds that they could Build Beautiful Swanky Fortresses, which might have 5,000 or more Advantages over whatever they now have, and without any Heating nor Cooling Bills. ‡

08-04 [_] O Selected King, if everyone in London had Stone Walls 10 or more feet THICK, it would Require 10 Times more Space for London: because the Houses are Back to Back and Side by Side with Tiny Garden Spaces.

08-05 [_] Well, you have to Remember my DESIGN, which calls for GIANT TERRACES, whereby all Buildings are Inside of those Terraces, and all Roofs are Covered with Fruit and Nut Trees, plus Vegetable and Flower Gardens: beCause there are many Advantages for Living in Beautiful Spacious Stone Dome Home Complexes, which have no Wasted Space for Streets, Parking Lots, Warehouses, Businesses, Houses, Tennis Courts, Gymnasiums, Swimming Pools, nor any other Buildings: because almost ALL of the Buildings are Underground, where they can take Advantage of the Consistent Temperatures of the Good Earth, which are FREE, which Saves TRILLIONS of Gallons of Gas, as well as tens of Trillions of Dollars, over Time. Indeed, many Americans are not Aware of how MUCH Fuel is Wasted while Heating and Cooling their Houses; but, it is an Average of about 6,000$ per Household per Year, TIMES 80 Million or so Houses, equals 480,000,000,000 Dollars per Year! And then we can Add on the Costs for Heating and Cooling Businesses, Schools, Churches, Theaters, Warehouses, Grocery Stores, Shopping Mauls, Factories, and so on — which adds up to more than ONE TRILLION DOLLARS per YEAR! †§‡

08-06 [_] So, O Elected King, are you saying that it might be Possible for us to SAVE a Trillion Dollars per Year, just by Building those **"GLORIOUS Swanky Hotels Castles and Fortresses!" (Beautiful Planned City States for WISE Intelligent Well-Educated People with Common Sense and Good Understanding!) By The Worldwide People's Revolution!® Book 019?**

08-07 [_] Well, Worldwide, it is Possible to Save tens of Trillions of Dollars by Building those Swanky Fortresses: beCause we are not the only Foolish nor Ignorant People who are Wasting lots of Energy, while Depriving ourselves of those Luscious Fruits, Nuts, and Vegetables. {See www.Amazon.com for: **"The LUSCIOUS All-Mineral Organic Method of Gardening!" (HOW to Grow DELICIOUS Satisfying Foods for Potential Kingz and Kweenz in Beautiful Swanky PALACES!) By The Worldwide People's Revolution!® Book 021.**}

08-08 [_] So, O Selected King, if we Act Wisely, we can still Save our Environment, and Reverse Global Warming, and Stop Acid Rains, and Free ourselves from all Debts, and Breathe Fresh Clean Air, once again, huh?

08-09 [_] Well, what are the Chances of Billions of People Deciding to Move into Self-air-conditioned UNDERGROUND Beautiful Stone Dome Home Complexes, with FREE Electricity, when they would much Prefer to Slave Away their Lives for Greedy Selfish Bankers, Gas Companies, the Electric Power Companies, Drug Companies, Tax Masters, and Government Bloodhounds? Indeed, they LOVE their Taxes, Insurance Bills, Doctor Bills, Hospital Bills, Telephone Bills, TV Bills, Water Bills, Car Payments, Mortgages, College Loan Debts, and so on:

beCause it is "the American Way": beCause of "the American Dream," which is a Great Self-deception: beCause it is Actually the Great American NIGHTMARE! Yes, it can be Proven in a Courtroom. †§‡§§

08-10 [_] So, O Selected King, what are some of the other "Sins of Capitalism," which most People do not Stop to Think about?

{FOOTNOTE: I had to Stop and Check some Potatoes, which were Boiling on the Gas Stove. So, after Discovering that those Potatoes were "Done," I turned the Gas from "Low" to "High," and then walked away, if you can Believe it? However, 3 Steps later, the still small Voice that Speaks with my "Conscience," or perhaps with my "Mind," said: "You had better Check the Stove," which I did. Otherwise, those Potatoes would have been "Cremated": beCause I Live at the other End of the 7,000 square-foot House, and therefore would not have Smelled them Burning, until it was too Late. And that is just another "Sin" of Capitalism: beCause it Teaches People to be "Independent." And I am the Last Person on the Earth that should be "Independent": beCause I am just Naturally an Interdependent Person, being like yourself: beCause there is no such an EVIL THING as Independence: beCause everyone and everything Depends on other People, Creatures, Plants, Sunlight, GOD and THINGS. Prove me to be WRong, if you can. Otherwise, Agree with me 100%, and Teach that same Great Truth to all of your Children, Friends, Naaberz, and whomever might have Spiritual Ears that can Hear, who might be Humble and Honest enough to Confess it. See www.Amazon.com for: **"The Low Court of Supreme Injustices is Brought to Trial!" (Our Elected King Butts Heads with the United States Supreme Court, with or without their Black Robes of Hypocrisies and Lies!) By The Worldwide People's Revolution!®**, Book 011, which contains the Famous *"Declaration of Interdependence,"* which you should also Read Aloud in any Open-minded Churches, Mosques, Synagogues, Cathedrals, Temples, Tabernacles, Bars, Ball Parks, Courthouses, Jails, Prisons, Hospitals, or wherever Honest Trustworthy People might be Discovered. See also: **"Thu Nq MAGNUFIID Verzhun uv Thu PROVERBZ uv KING SOLUMUN in Plaan Ingglish!" (The Understandable Version of the Famous Proverbs of King Solomon in Plain English!) By The Worldwide People's Revolution!® Book 028.**}

— Chapter 09 —

"You shall Know them by their Fruits"

09-01 [_] Jesus said, *"You shall Know the Health of Trees by their Fruits. Indeed, a Healthy Tree cannot Produce Diseased Fruits, neither can a Diseased Tree Produce Healthy Fruits. Likewise, you shall Know what Kind of People they are by their Fruits, or Works: because Good People do not Produce Evil Works; but, it is possible for Evil People to Produce what Appears to be Good Works: because they are Deceptive People, who cannot be Trusted. Therefore, you must Inspect all of their Fruits, in Order to Judge them Correctly. For Example, there will Arise an Evil Empire during the Last Days, before my Second Coming, which will be doing many Evil Deeds in the Names of Freedom, Liberty, Democracy, and Justice for ALL, which will be very Hypocritical. However, most People will be Extremely Ignorant at that Time, in spite of going to Schools, where they will be Indoctrinated with all Kinds of Deceptions and Lies: because Satan is in Charge of them, being their Master, which is why that I call it the Synagogue of Satan: because it will be a Religious Political Military Industrial Bankers' Complex, being Managed by Rich Red Jew Bankers and many other Edomite Masters, who will have Control of the News Media, Book Publishing Companies, Movie Productions, and Especially Drug Businesses, which will be their Primary Source of Financial Gain: because Multitudes of Ignorant People will be Addicted to their Drugs, which they will Imagine keeps them Healthy. Indeed, nothing could be farther from the Truth: because none of the Wild Animals use any such Drugs, and almost all of them are Healthier and Happier than most People: because they are Free with a Capital F, while People are Addicted with a Capital A."* — The White Jew's Version †§‡

09-02 [_] O Selected King, what you are saying is True; but, it is NOT *Scriptural:* because the *Bible* does not make any such Statement, even if it should. Therefore, it is just another LIE. †§‡

09-03 [_] Well, you will have to Confess that it is a Harmless Deception: beCause I do not Pretend that it comes from the *Bible;* but, it comes from some White Jew, who has his own Personal Translations of all such Things, which are likely just as Good, or even Better, than any other Translations. Indeed, God will have to be the Judge of that. Meanwhile, did you Consider the Great Truths within that Verse? Have you Noticed that Sick Diseased People cannot Produce Healthy Happy Children? Are you Aware that Healthy Babies do not Cry. Indeed, that was HOW the Parents of Moses could Hide him in the Bulrushes for 3 Months without anyone Noticing it, including the Alligators and Egyptian Crocodiles: beCause he did not Cry, nor Stink!

09-04 [_] O Selected King, you have got to be Kidding us! There is no Way that Moses' Parents could have Hidden Moses in Bulrushes for 3 Months without someone Detecting it. By the way, just Exactly WHERE were those Bulrushes in Egypt? Are you not Aware that Egypt was Paved with Streets of Gold at that Time? I Mean that all of the Streets around the Capital Buildings were Paved with Pure Gold, which the Biblical Authors were Unaware of: beCause they never Visited Egypt! In Fact, the Great Pyramid was also Plated with Pure Gold, from Top to Bottom, and had a Crowning Pyramid about 3 feet high, which was Solid Gold! And that is WHY that Pyramid was Stripped Naked, later on, whereby the Robbers even took away the Limestone Facing that Covered it: beCause of being too Lazy to Quarry their own Limestone Rocks. Indeed, the same thing

Happened in Mexico, when the Gold was Stripped Off of the Pyramids of the Sun and Moon by the Conquerors, who should have Respected them as a Civilized Society. But, instead, they Plundered them, and did not even Report it in Spain. Nevertheless, they used much of that Gold to Decorate their countless Churches throughout Mexico, which was Better than Hiding it in Bank Vaults, deep in the Ground, under New Yuck City, where no one gets to Enjoy it, which is another SIN of Capitalism. †§‡

09-05 [_] Well, I have no Idea WHERE the Bulrushes were Located; but, it is Unlikely that Pharaoh had Alligators anywhere around his Palaces, lest the Children should be Eaten by them; and Bulrushes would have been Perfect Places for Crocodiles to Hide among. However, according to the Jewish Myth, the Children of Israel were Settled in the Land of GOSHEN, which was a long ways from Pharaoh's Palaces. Moreover, they supposedly Built Treasure Cities for Pharaoh, which have yet to be Discovered. Ramesses the Great was supposedly Drowned in the Red Sea, along with 600 Iron Chariots; but, according to *Wikipedia,* Ramesses II Lived for 90—91 Years, and was Buried in the Valley of the Kings, and was Discovered in 1881, and is now on Display in a Cairo Museum. It is Interesting to Note that his Father, Seti I, means a "Descendant of Seth," who was the Son of Adam with Red Hairs, even as Ramesses II had Red Hairs, and even as I also have Red Hairs, which was also True of George Washington and Thomas Jefferson: beCause there is something Special about us Redheads, whether or not anyone Likes it. ‡

09-06 [_] So, O Selected King, was Mark Twain also a Redhead?

09-07 [_] Absolutely, and so was Michelangelo, Leonardo da Vinci, William Shakespeare, Henry David Thoreau, and Jesus Christ, himself! Yes, it can be Proven in a Courtroom, if anyone is Interested in it. †‡

09-08 [_] O Selected King, perhaps that is what is WRong with Capitalism — which was an Invention of Redheaded Jews, who were gone Astray from the Path of Life, Lost in the Darkness of Ignorance, Buried in Intellectual Garbage, and Covered with Great Shame! Yes, what a Bad Legacy to leave behind. Therefore, why in the World would you Want to be Associated with all such EVIL People?

09-09 [_] Well, I never did Want to be Associated with any of them: beCause I Calculated that I was Better than any of them from the Beginning — long before any of us were Born! However, God has Informed me that Jesus Christ was Far Better than I am, which is Good: beCause, if he was not, we would all be in BIG Trouble! After all, it is most Difficult to Compete with Jewish Mythologies, which are Constructed from the Point of View of a Humble Honest Peasant, you might say — such as a Farmer, Stone Mason, or even the Son of a Butcher, who has Empathy for all such Poor Creatures, who can Relate with: *"Blest are the Meek, Teachable People: beCause they will Inherit the Earth, not Heaven."* (See *Matthew 5.*)

09-10 [_] O Selected King, Capitalism has Proven itself to be a FARCE, or a First Class CHARADE, which Forever Boasts about the Great Successes of a few Rich Hogs, who took Advantages of the Masses of Ignorant People, who never Heard of a RIGHTEOUS One-World GovernMINT: beCause Capitalism Avoids that Important Subject. Therefore, the Masses of People never Learn about it, much less Think about it, until they Visualize the Beauty of it with a Capital B, whereby almost everyone in the World could become Moderately Rich, just by their

(A List of the EVILS of CAPITALISM!)

Honest Labors, alone, without any Bankers, without any Loans, without any Interest Slavery, and without any Tax Slavery. Indeed, it is all so Simple that they cannot Comprehend it: beCause their Minds have been Muddled Up by Capitalists, who Complicate everything as much as Possible, who use PRIDE to Blinds the Minds of Ignorant Fools, who cannot Understand the SIMPLICITY of a Righteous One-World GovernMINT, which simply Mints and Prints the Necessary New Money — NOT to give it away to Ignorant Fools, nor to Waste it on Bank Robbers; but, in Order to Use that New Money WISELY, in Order to HIRE whomever is Willing and Able to Learn and Work, in Order to Help Build **"GLORIOUS Swanky Hotels Castles and Fortresses!" (Beautiful Planned City States for WISE Intelligent Well-Educated People with Common Sense and Good Understanding!)**, Book 019, which Fortresses Represent that New Money, which makes it the very Best Money in all of the World: beCause it must be EARNED by Honest Labor, without any Loans, without any Usury, and without any Taxes! Yes, Strangely enough, those Tax Slaves can read that Sentence no less than 100 Times, and still cannot Visualize what it MEANS: beCause of having their Minds WARPED by **"The Public School of IGNERUNT FQLZ!" (HOW we have been GRAATLEE DISEEVD by Capitalism!)**, Book 024: beCause that School has its Head Stuck in one or the other of those 2 Stinking Holes in: **"The BIG White OUTHOUSE on the Not-so-Biblical Capitol DUNGHILL!" (The Chief Sins of the Divided States of United Lies!)**, Book 023, which is a most Painful Book to "reed," when you Reject the most Simple Truths — such as the Truths about the Evil Events of September 11th, 2001, which are Supported by Scientific Facts. For Example, there were 3 Great Towers that came Crashing Down during that Day, and one of them was not Struck by any Airplane, which actually had a larger Base than Towers 1 or 2, which was Tower 7, which was 47 Stories Tall, having 283 Hardened Steel Columns in it (many of which were 22-inches by 52-inches, and 47 stories tall), which all Decided to come Crashing Down in less than 7 Seconds without the Use of any EXPLOSIVES, if you can Believe it!? Yes, the National Institute of Sciences and Technologies (NIST) Believes it: beCause their Computers PROVED it. Yes, all of the Data was Fed into their Computers, except for the Eyewitnesses Testimonies of 250+ Firemen, who were never Questioned by NIST: beCause, "there was nothing scientific about their testimonies," even though they all Unanimously Agreed that they Heard LOUD EXPLOSIONS throughout Building 7 before it Collapsed! In other Words, there must have been LOTS of Explosives Set Up in Tower 7, WEEKS in Advance of September 11th, 2001: beCause, not even David Copperfield could have pulled off such a Magician's Trick as that, much less Osama bin Obama, Incorporated, who had absolutely nothing to do with it. But, George Warmonger Bush and Little Dick Chicanery, Incorporated, must have had MUCH to do with it: beCause they Impeded any Thorough Investigation into the Crime, until Years Later, after all of the Physical Evidences were Destroyed as much as was Possible. However, certain Wise People kept the Remains of the Dust that Settled all over Manhattan, which can still be Studied in Laboratories, if anyone Cares to do so, which Dust contains much Proof that Explosives were Used in all 3 Towers! Yes, it can be Proven in a Courtroom, O Tax Slaves, if anyone is Interested in True JUSTICE with a Capital J. However, I See that only a very Small Percentage of Americans are Interested: beCause of having their Heads STUCK in one or the other of those 2 Stinking Holes in the Big White OUTHOUSE, in Washington, District of Chief Criminals! †§‡§§ (See the many Links on www.AE911TRUTH.org for Mountains of PROOF! Follow the Links to Dr. Judy Wood on YouTube Videos for more Proof. Google: **Experts Speak Out,** for much Proof of what I Teach, and Understand that X-amount of Edomites got RICH from those False Flag Operations! Yes, *the Love of Money* was Behind the Scenes of those Crimes.)

— Chapter 10 —

Capitalist Lies by the Dozen!

10-01 [_] We are told in the School of Fools that if we go to school, get a good education, work hard, save our money, and play by the rules, we are bound to succeed in life. No Mention is made of Bankers' Recessions, Great Depressions, Terrorist Attacks, Failing Stock Markets, Bloody Wars, Droughts, Famines, Fires, Tornadoes, Hurricanes, Earthquakes, Mudslides, Floods, nor other Natural and Unnatural Disasters: beCause all such Capitalists live in an "American Dream," where all is Well, even if all is Hell. Yes, they call it "Optimism," "a Positive Mind," "Positive Thinking," and so on. However, as with Individual Persons, whole Nations can go to Hell by such Ways and Means: beCause of Ignoring **"The Seven Basic Spiritual Building Blocks of LIFE!" (Faith, Hope, Trust, Love, Patience, Persistence and OBEDIENCE!)**, Book 036. Indeed, there is more to "Success" than just being "Positive-minded." After all, you could Drive your Car on the WRong Side of the Freeway: beCause of being Positive-minded, while Knowing for a FACT that you are Headed in the Correct Direction, even while Crashing Head-on into a Semi-Truck Loaded with Heavy Steel I-Beams for Building a Bridge across the Atlantic Ocean, which Rests on Used Oil Drums, which might Work Well, until the Drums RUST OUT, and the Bridge SINKS to the Bottom of the Sea! Yes, it is the POWER of "Positive Thinking" without any Common Sense! And such was the Construction of Atomic Power Plants, which Produce Radioactive DUNG, which no one knows WHERE to Store: beCause it is not Safe to be around for any less than 25 Million Years! Moreover, that was Known long before they made the First Atomic ElecTRICK Power Plant, and yet the CONgress Passed the Bills, and made it all Possible: beCause of being "educated" with a Lower-case e. †‡

10-02 [_] O Selected King, was the General Public not Informed about all such Abominations before they were Produced? Was it not put on the Ballot for an Election?

10-03 [_] Well, it is for Certain that X-amount of People knew about it; but, as with almost all Greedy Capitalist Enterprises, the General Public was not made to Understand the Hateful Consequences of Meddling with Satan's Toys: beCause those Red Jew Bankers Gained BILLIONS of Dollars by making Loans to those Nations that Bought into the Big Lie about Cheap ElecTrickery and "Pollution-free" ElecTrickery, called "Clean Energy," which is like Clean Cancers, Fragrant Abscesses, Non-stinking Outhouses, Odorless Chicken Farms, and Sanitary Hog Factory Farms. Yes, all such Capitalist Lies come by the Dozen; but, not for Free: beCause someone must Pay the COSTS. And the Final Costs for Radioactive Dung could be World War 3: beCause X-amount of People in this World do not Like to be LIED to, including myself. However, I would not be the Unholy One to Push the Big Red Button: beCause I have more Common Sense than to do an Evil Thing like that; but, ISIS (Israeli Secret Instigation Services) is quite well Able to Do that, and without a Bad Conscience — even as they Beat Down Ancient Monuments in Syria with Sledge Hammers: beCause of Forgetting the Laws of MOSES, who said to not Destroy the Ancient Landmarks, which would Include those Ancient Monuments. (See *Deuteronomy 19:14; 27:17; Proverbs **22:28; 23:10** and Hosea 5:10.*)

(A List of the EVILS of CAPITALISM!)

10-04 [_] O Selected King, it seems that Capitalism runs Roughshod over DUMBmocracy, which should have a Vote concerning all such Evil Things: beCause WHO Wants to Inherit the Wind, which is apt to Blow Away?

10-05 [_] Well, DUMBmocracy is just a Powerless JOKE, if you ask me, which is used to Deceive Ignorant People, who seldom get to Vote concerning any Specific Issue that might be of Great Importance to them, which would not be the Case, if they were Living within those **"GLORIOUS Swanky Hotels Castles and Fortresses!" (Beautiful Planned City States for WISE Intelligent Well-Educated People with Common Sense and Good Understanding!) By The Worldwide People's Revolution!® **Book 019. Indeed, each Planned City State would Govern itself According to its own Elected Laws and Flexible Rules, even if they Wanted to Marry Cows, Hogs, Dogs, Horses, or whatever: beCause that would be THEIR Business, not mine. ‡

10-06 [_] So, O Selected King, are you saying that you do not Object to GAY Marriages? Will all such Marriages not Destroy a Nation much more Quickly than Atomic Electric Power Plants and Guided Missiles?

10-07 [_] Well, would you rather have Young Men Whoring around Town, Bar Hopping, and Jumping into Bed with any Skunk that they might Find, whereby HIV-AIDS has been Spread all around the World; or, would you not rather have them get Married, and Practice FIDELITY? God much Prefers Fidelity, which is WHY many of those "Gay Lovers" will Enter into the Kingdom of God LONG before those Adulterers, Fornicators, Divorcees, and Liars. Indeed, David and Jonathan will Enter into the Kingdom of God Long before Bill Adulterous Lying Clinton, for Example: beCause God has no Use for Infidelity, and neither do I. In Fact, that is Precisely WHY that I have never gotten Married to anyone: beCause I Believe in FIDELITY, and I have never Discovered anyone else who Believes in it, who might be Qualified to Marry me. So, I have Lived a Lonely and Deprived Life beCause of my Beliefs, for which God will have to Honor me during the Judgment Day: beCause it has not been Easy to Live such a Life, nor was it Necessary: beCause everyone should Believe in FIDELITY. ‡

10-08 [_] So, O Selected King, did Capitalism bring all of that about, or what? Was it Capitalism that Caused hundreds of millions of All-American Divorces, or what??

10-09 [_] Well, I would say that Capitalism was the Primary Cause for almost all of those Divorces: beCause the Love of Money Causes People to Say and Do Strange Things. {See www.Amazon.com on the Internet: **"For the Love of Money!" (The Strange Things that People Say and Do to Get more Money!) By The Worldwide People's Revolution!®** Book 003.}

10-10 [_] O Selected King, I have no Idea HOW you could Live for 70+ Years without someone to LOVE, even if she were some Painted Highly-perfumed SKUNK, as you might call her, who could take a Shower with Gasoline, and then Wash herself with LIE-sol, and then Disinfect herself with DDT, and at last Drink some Battery Acid, just to Kill the WORMS within her! †§‡

— Chapter 11 —

The Power of Advertisements

11-01 [_] You have probably Noticed that there are "countless" Advertisements on Televisions around the World: beCause they have Proven to be Profitable, in spite of Producing X-amount of Food Addicts, Drug Addicts, Alcoholics, Gluttons, Obese Walruses, Sickly Coke Children, and so on. Indeed, all such Advertisements are LEGAL, even as it was Legal to Advertise Tobacco Products for a hundred Years, or more, until it was Proven that such Products Cause Cancers, whereby Protesters Persuaded Politicians to Limit the Advertisements, who could have simply Outlawed the Use of all such Tobacco Products; but, behold, all such Products have been a Major Source of Revenue for Tax Masters, including Alcoholic Beverages, which were once Outlawed in the Divided States of United Lies, which Drove the Addicts Underground with Jesus Christ, who Transformed the Water into Wine, according to *John 4:* beCause he Knew that People Needed some "Happy Water," just to Cheer them Up, now and then. Yes, he Understood the Necessity for DRUGS, also, which is WHY he said: †§‡

11-02 [_] *"When you get Sick or Diseased, do not Fast nor Pray, as Job and King David did; but, go to the Witchdoctor, and get yourself some Drugs: beCause only Drugs can Heal you. Indeed, my Father Joseph once Cut himself with the Drawknife when he was making a Chair Leg, and Mary Sewed Up the Wound with a Needle and Thread, after Sterilizing it with some Whiskey, which was made from Barley; and then the Wound was Anointed with some of that Whiskey, which Sterilized it; and then she Anointed it with some Fresh Olive Oil, in order to Sooth the Burning Sensation from the Whiskey, whereby the Pain was Relieved. And behold, within a few Days the Wound was completely Healed up: beCause Joseph did not Eat nor Drink anything for one Week, which Worked like Magic, you might say. However, a Naaber sed that he should at least go to the Witchdoctor, and have him Inspect it for any Infections, and perhaps take some Drugs to Cure it; but, Joseph Refused, saying that his Body had the Capability to Heal itself, which it did. And then we got a TV, after that, which kept Advertising all Kinds of Drugs and Medicines and Remedies for this and for that, while Warning us about Bad Side Effects, and especially if those Drugs were Consumed with Alcoholic Drinks, which might even Cause Heart Attacks, Strokes, Aneurysms, and even Deaths. Nevertheless, being Weak-minded, Mary did not Listen to the Good Advice of her Husband, whereby she Bought into the Big Lie, which was Promoted by the Roman Government, which Received Taxes from the Sales of all such Drugs, whereby they did not Outlaw any of those Drugs: beCause they could not Prove by any Means that the Drugs were Causing all nor any of those other Ailments; and therefore, being a Daughter of Deceptions, ever since the Garden of Eden Episode, she just Naturally got herself a Bottle of Peptoobizmuk, which seemed to be rather Harmless, until she started having Symptoms of other Ailments, whereupon the Witchdoctor Advised that she should use this or that other MediSIN, whereby she Naturally Contracted more and more Ailments, which Required more and more Drugs, until at Last Poor Old Joseph found himself in a Profound State of Poverty: beCause of Buying so many Drugs. Yes, he had to Mortgage his House to Friendly Bankers, just to get Enough Money for Buying those Countless Pills, which were made mostly of White Refined Sugar, which alone could Cause an Imbalance in a Person's Immune System.*

(A List of the EVILS of CAPITALISM!)

11-03 [_] *"Now, it came to pass that Poor Old Joseph Died from the Stress of it all, and the Bankers Collected his House: beCause all of us Sons had gone out and Sold all that we had, and Distributed our Wealth among the Poor People in Jerusalem: beCause there are Countless Poor People in all such Cities of Confusion: beCause none of them were ever Designed for Living, except Ancient Babylon, which had Beautiful Hanging Gardens: because the whole City was Built in large Terraces, having all of the Houses Inside of those Terraces, with the Fruit Trees and Gardens on Top of their Roofs: because King Neb was one of the Wisest of Men who ever Lived, who was the Head of Gold in Daniel's Dream, if you Recall. Yes, King Neb knew all about the Grand Deceptions of Witchdoctors, and how that they have Countless Potions and Endless False Notions about Good Health. Nevertheless, being Poor and Ignorant, my Mother Mary was Forced to GIVE UP her MediSINZ, and take up Fasting and Praying with Anna, in the Temple, which had Special Beds and Toilets for the Purpose of Fasting, which was Designed by King Solomon: because he Understood the Importance of Fasting, Periodically: beCause it Allows the Body and Mind to Cleanse itself of any Impurities, including those Addictive Drugs. Therefore, after a Month or 2 of Fasting and Praying, my Mother Recovered, and then she Decided that it was Best for her to come Follow after me: beCause Rome did not Offer any Welfare Assistance at that Time, being Destitute for more Money for making Wars against Heathen Tribes in all Directions, in Order to Civilize and Democratize them. After all, until Rome got into Power, People did not even have Paved Roads to Travel on with their Horses and Wagons; but, they just Followed Cow Trails and Goat Paths, you might say.* ‡

11-04 [_] *"So, it came to pass that MuhamMAD Suddenly Appeared one Day with the Cramps in his Bowels, Begging me to Heal him: beCause he had Heard that I was doing Miracles here and there as I Traveled all about, even to Arabia, where MuhamMAD had Flown in on his Horse with 4 Wings, each of which was about 2 feet long, if you can Believe it? Indeed, I told his Teacher that I did not Believe it; but, he Assured me that it was True, and that People have been known to Fly up to Heaven on Prayer Rugs, if they just Chant the same Prayer, over and over, 10 Times or more per Day, to Allah: because it Worked for those Hindus and Buddhists, also. Nevertheless, I told them that I was not Interested in any such Nonsense, for which Reason they were about to Stone me to Death: beCause of Worshiping some Ignorant Fool like MuhamMAD, who could not even Reed nor Riit, much less Fly into the Sky on some Winged Horse, who would need Wings no less than 40 feet across, just to Carry the Weight of the Horse, alone, even if he were Skinny. But, to also Carry the Weight of a Maniac on his Back, his Wings would have to be at least 60 feet across with Oxygen Tanks Installed on them. However, rather than Allow those Ignorant Fools to Stone me to Death, I just Slipped into a Tent, and Turned my Robe Inside Out, and went Out on the Backside of it, and Disappeared among the Crowd with a Veil over my Head, and thus got Out of that Hateful Place. After all, why should a Man Die by the Hands of Fools, when he can more Properly Die at the Hands of Wise Scribes and Pharisees?*

11-05 [_] *"Yes, I have Contemplated it many Times — asking myself just Exactly what would be the most Appropriate Way for a Holy Man to DIE? After all, being Sacrificed on some Fiery Altar is not all that Appealing: beCause of being Roasted to Death, while still Alive and in my Riit Miind. Therefore, I Persuaded those Romans that the Best Way for me to Die would be on a Torture Stake, whereby I might be Able to Resurrect myself, if I were not Totally Dead, which seemed to be Reasonable enough to them. After all, most Crucified Men Live for at least 3 to 7 Days while Hanging on a Cross. Therefore, if I could Die within just one Day, I might be Well enough to be Healed, and thus Arise from the Dead — that is, from what would be Believed to be the Dead:*

beCause no one on the whole Earth would Believe that a Person could be Whipped and Beaten and Kicked in the Groin and Mocked and Spit upon and Tormented so much, and at last Arise from the Dead, after being Crucified! But, that is Exactly what Happened: because I was Fasting and Praying the whole Time, and even a Week beforehand: beCause I Understood the POWER of a Body to Heal itself. Therefore, what seemed to be very Miraculous to Ignorant People was Actually just a Natural Thing for a Young Man like me, who was in the Prime of his Life. Moreover, my 'Resurrection' had to be brought about, just to 'Fulfill' Prophecies! Therefore, do not Think of it as a Strange Thing, nor Imagine that it was some Grand Deception — such as the Drug Industry Practices: beCause the Body is Actually Able and Willing to Heal itself, if we just Cooperate with it, which is HOW I Managed to get myself Up from the 'Dead,' even though I was not Actually Dead; but, just as Good as Dead: beCause I was near unto Death, and certainly was Walking through the Valley of the Shadow of Death with King David, who Visualized my 'Death and Resurrection.' Yes, you need to Study Psalm 22 and 23 again: beCause I am still Alive and Well. Yes, I am Impersonating the Selected King of **The Worldwide People's Revolution!**®, *himself, you might say: beCause I am Inspiring him to Write all of these Words, whereby Worldly-wise People will be Greatly Confounded: beCause they will not be Able to Understand all such Words; but, the Righteous People will Understand, and the Most Holy Ones will FLY AWAY on the Wings of a Great Eagle, you might say, even unto Mount Zion, which is Inside of the Hollow Earth, just as it is written in Psalms 48, 50, and 87. Yes, it Requires much Faith to Believe that; but, when your Life Depends on Escaping, you will get Desperate, and you will also Help other Believers to Escape: beCause it will Require the United Effort of all of the Believers to Escape. Therefore, Pray to God that you are Accounted Worthy to Escape, and thus Help to Spread this Good News far and wide: so that all of the Believers might Learn about it, and thus Help themselves and others to Escape: beCause the Believers are Scattered Out all around the World, just to Test your Faith in my Inspired Words of Provable Truths."* — The Peacock Version †§‡§§

11-06 [_] O Selected King, I Swear to God that in all of my Life, I have never Heard any Words so Ridiculous as those Words! You cannot be Serious! Moreover, why do you HIDE all such Words in a Book like this, when you could write a much Better Book, called: **"HOW the True Church will Escape from the Great Tribulation!" (The Secret City of the Great King!) By The Worldwide People's Revolution!®** Book 042?

11-07 [_] Well, that would all Depend on just WHICH WORDS that you are Referring to? After all, there are a LOT of Truths within those Words, which you must now DIVIDE or Separate within the Belly of your own Mind. Yes, like the *Bible,* you must Learn to Separate the Truths from the Lies, both of which are Obvious to Educated People.

11-08 [_] So, O Selected King, just how MANY Books do you Intend to Sell to us? Are you not another Greedy Capitalist?

11-09 [_] Well, if you read the Copyright Pages in my Books, you will Discover that anyone may Sell my Books, and KEEP 90% of the Net Profits for their own Prosperity. Therefore, I would say that I am rather Generous, and not at all Greedy by any Means. However, I am Sure that X-amount of Ignorant People will be Falsely Accusing me of being GREEDY, even though I am probably the most Generous Person that they have ever Heard of! After all, I Offer every Willing and Able-bodied Person in the Whole World a Beautiful Swanky PALACE to Live in, if they Want to, and only for 4 Hours of Common Skilled Labor per Day, or the Equivalent thereof, and only for 6

Years of Labor, without any Loans, without any Interest, and without any Taxes. Therefore, HOW can anyone Beat on that Plan with an Ugly Stick? {See www.Amazon.com for: **"SWANGKEENOMIKS Rules the Roost!" (HOW all People can Prosper in a RIIT WAA, and STOP Polluting the Earth with Capitalist TRASH!) By The Worldwide People's Revolution!®** Book 039.}

11-10 [_] O Selected King, before the True Church can Escape, she must become HOLY, which she is not likely to Do while reading all such Twisted Words as you are able to write. In Fact, she would have to Do a LOT of Fasting, just to get her Mind Cleaned Up enough to Comprehend all such Words, which make no Sense to an Unenlightened Person, who might Understand what it Means to ADVERTISE Drugs, Cars, and other Abominations; but, to Understand Spiritual Things, a Person must Study: **"The Seven Basic Spiritual Building Blocks of LIFE!" (Faith, Hope, Trust, Love, Patience, Persistence and OBEDIENCE!)**, Book 036, which is so Deep and Dark as to be another Mystery, itself! Therefore, I am now Thinking that you do not stand a Chance of Discovering so many as 500 People to Fly Away to Mount Zion in a Blimp, much less in an Airplane, which is Powered by Jet Fuel, which is another Abomination, which Holy People would not go near, much less Use it to Escape from Babylon, the Great Mother / Producer of Prostitutes and Abominations. Therefore, I am Greatly Confused by your Master Plan, which is not Understandable, which is Full of Sarcasms and Double-speak and all such Orwellian Nonsense. Yes, I must Confess that the "Hand of God" is most Likely Dealing with you: beCause it is his Strange Way of Operating, even as it was since the Beginning, whereby he might Discover the WISEST People for Governing his Great Kingdom, who would also have to be the Most HONEST People, and the Most Diligent People, who have Studied the *Scriptures* with Open Minds: beCause it is True that not all of those Words can be Trusted, even as you have Proven within your Inspired Books, which also cannot be Trusted. However, once a Person Discovers the Whole Truth, it is easy to Separate the Truths from the Lies, and thus Learn to Love the Whole Truth, which is Scattered Out within all of your Inspired Books: so that only a Select FEW People will Escape and be Saved for Positions within the Holy Kingdom of All that is GOOD. Therefore, I will Cling Tightly to your *Rope of Hope,* and be Patient with Persistence and OBEDIENCE: beCause there is no other Way to be Blest, nor Happy! Yes, we must Trust and OBEY. †§‡

— Chapter 12 —

Capitalism Produces Great STRESS!

12-01 [_] Just Think of how Difficult it would be to Lose your Job, if you Lived in a Glorious Swanky Fortress, and had your own Private and LUSCIOUS All-Mineral Organic Garden, Vineyard, and Orchard with a Home-craft Workshop and Sales Shop, along with all of the Necessary Well-made Tools to Work with, including Canning Tools for Storing Up thousands of Jars of Fruit Juices and Various Kinds of Vegetable Soups, Condensed Soups, and Canned Fruits: so that you would be Guaranteed to have LOTS of Good Foods, even if a Great Drought should come. Indeed, you could have Tons of Dried Fruits — such as Dates and Figs and Nuts — in your Walk-in Cooler and Freezer, which can be Stored Well for a hundred Years or more! However, in the Capitalist System, you are at the Mercy of the Gross Grocery Stores, which are about as Reliable as the ElecTrickery, which can go Off at any Time: beCause of Trees falling on Power Lines in Ice Storms, Wind Storms, Tornadoes, Hurricanes, Fires, Floods, and whatever. However, at a Swanky Fortress, there would be no Exposed Power Lines to fall down: beCause they would all be Inside of Secure Tunnels, along with all Means of Transportation, Plumbing Pipes, TV Cables, Internet, and whatever. ‡

12-02 [_] So, O Elected King, with such Secure Fortresses, HOW would anyone Learn to FEAR God, who is the Creator of all of those Evil Tornadoes, Hurricanes, Fires, Floods, and whatever? Would People not get PUFFED UP with Great PRIDE: beCause of being Healthy and RICH? ‡

12-03 [_] Well, I suppose that they could get Puffed Up with Great Pride, and Especially if they were not Taught the Truth about God, who is the Creator of all GOOD Things, while Satan is the Inventor of all EVIL Things, including those Tornadoes and Hurricanes, which have no Goodness in them at all, while Fire and Water can at least be used Wisely for Good Purposes, and also be Controlled. †§‡

12-04 [_] So, O Selected King, are you saying that Satan Created Mosquitoes, while God Created the Birds that Eat Mosquitoes??

12-05 [_] Well, that is Disputable, since God Supposedly Created ALL Things, including Mosquitoes, Malaria, Ticks, Tick Fevers, Chiggers, Itches, Fleas, Bedbugs, Lice, Weevils, Mice, Rats, Snakes, Drugs, Skunks, Prostitutes, Politicians and whatever. (See *John 1* for the Proof.) However, it makes no Sense that God would Love his Children by Creating Mosquitoes and Malaria, Scarlet Fever, Diphtheria, Smallpox, and a Million other Sicknesses and Diseases: beCause that seems to be a little CRUEL, would you not say? ‡

12-06 [_] O Selected King, it is easy to Understand WHY some People call themselves Atheists: beCause the *Biblical* God makes no Sense.

12-07 [_] Well, it could be that the Biblical God is nothing but Jewish Mythology, since there is much Evidence of it, and hardly anything to Support such a Mythical God, other than a Vast Universe with Trillions of Worlds, which no one God could Possibly Care for. †§‡

12-08 [_] So, O Selected King, if you do not Believe in the *Biblical God,* whose God do you Believe in?

12-09 [_] Well, I Firmly Believe in a Great Creator God: beCause it is Impossible to have Laws without a Lawmaker. Moreover, I also Firmly Believe in a God of Justice, which does not Fit in with the *Biblical God of Injustices* — such as the Canaanite Genocide, which never got carried out, anyway: beCause nobody else Believed in it, including God. However, if he did Believe in it, he could have Killed all of those Canaanites, himself, rather than make Murderers of the Israelites, who did not Need nor Want that Burden of Guilt to Bear. Indeed, ISIS (Israeli Secret Instigation Services) would also have their Consciences Racked for their Murders, if they Believed in the God of True Justice, who would never Ask anyone to Do such Evil Things. However, the Way that the *Bible* reads, one would Think that if you did NOT Murder those Canaanite Babies, by Dashing their Heads against Stone Walls, you would be DOOMED, which would also Cause Great STRESS, if your Conscience was Working Correctly, and might even Cause you to Commit Suicide for Doing such EVIL Things. Therefore, Jesus came along with a New Plan, which was to get them Converted to the Truth, and even Sacrifice your own Life to Save their Lives, whereby Missionaries were Born. ‡

12-10 [_] O Selected King, the Bible is Extremely Frustrating, if you Stop to Think about its Contradictions; but, I Prefer to NOT Think about anything that Upsets me: beCause it is Better for me to Live in a Dream World, according to my own Great Imagination. For Example, Jesus was supposedly the LORD God of the *Old Testament,* who Commanded Moses to Murder all of those Canaanites, Hittites, Hivites, Jebuzites, Lamanites, Mennonites, and whatever else was over there in the Promised Land: beCause, he is the SAME, both Yesterday, Today and Forever, even an Unchangeable God from all of Eternity to all of Eternity: beCause he was Living before his Father in Heaven: beCause ALL Things, including the Father God, was Created by JESUS CHRIST, just as the Apostle Paul Confirmed, saying that he Created ALL Things in Heaven and on Earth, which Means that he Created Orion and all of the Stars, and then got Lonely, and thus Decided to come Down here and let Idiots Crucify him: so that he could Rightfully Rule Over them. However, you and I had nothing to do with his Crucifixion; and therefore, how can he Rightfully Rule Over US? Indeed, Capitalist Businesses might put People into Great STRESS; but, what can be as Stressful as *Bible Study?* †§‡ (See: *John 1; Colossians 1:16; Ephesians 3:9; and Revelation 4:11, KJV.*)

12-11 [_] Well, I do not Allow it to get me Stressed by any Means: beCause I Know for a Fact that it must be the Concoction of some Lying Red Jews, who alone could Invent such Nonsense: beCause no Thinking Person would ever come up with such Fantasies. However, it could be that Zealots just left Out a few Important Words, and also Added a few Unimportant words. For Example, it could be that all Good Things in this World, on this Earth, were in Fact Created by Jesus Christ, or at least According to his Desires: beCause that is Believable. But, the Idea that he Created ALL Things in the Vast Heavens above / below, and all around, is a bit Ridiculous: beCause those Stars have been there for Billions of Years, while Jesus has been around for about 2,000 Years, being Born from Mary, according to the *Bible,* which is most likely Correct about that Part of the Story; but, as for a Virgin Birth, that is Debatable. Many Ancient Mythical Characters were also Born from Virgins, and did Miracles, and even Arose from the Dead after 3 Days. (See the Internet for *Zeitgeist Videos.*) Ancient Literature is full of all such Mythologies.

The Nature of CAPITALISM!

12-12 [_] O Selected King, a Person could easily Lose Faith in the *Holy Bible:* beCause of all such Words. Therefore, is it GOOD to Teach Children to DOUBT the *Bible?* Will they not be Deprived of much True Knowledge, which could Help them throughout their Lives, if they should Learn them by Studying their Bibles?

12-13 [_] Well, I maintain that the *Bible* should be put on Trial, and Proven to be True or False, and thus Correct any Lies within it, or else at least have an Introduction that Explains HOW it was Constructed, and by WHOM it was Constructed, and WHY it is so Contradictory with Realities, seeing that no True God would be so Contradictory, nor Insane as to Lay Murder and Guilt on his Chosen People, who could never Live it down, who would be Driven Insane by GUILT. Yes, that is WHY so many Veterans Commit Suicide: beCause they are Racked with GUILT for their Murders of Innocent People, which is just a Natural Reaction to Evil Actions. ‡

12-14 [_] So, O Selected King, what about the Great STRESS of going to War to Fight for Capitalism — is that not a Great EVIL?

12-15 [_] Well, it has certainly made a lot of Young Men Gray Haired: beCause that Stress is no Good, which also Afflicts Presidents and Rulers all around the World, who Worry themselves over this or that, which would not be the Case within Swanky Fortresses: beCause no Bad People could get Into them; but, they could be Cast Out of them, if they were Born in them. Indeed, that would be the Ultimate Punishment, which would be a Dreadful Thing: beCause all such Banished People would have to Live in the Wilderness with Snakes, Skunks, Bears, Lions, Wolves, and whatever might be Out there to Torment them.

12-16 [_] O Selected King, would you Permit us to Smoke Marijuana in Swanky Fortresses?

12-17 [_] Well, when you Fill Out the SURVEYS of your VALUES, be Sure to Check the Appropriate Boxes, if you Want to Grow and Smoke Marijuana, or whatever: beCause it will not Bother me: beCause I will Choose to Live with People who are not Addicted to Weeds, who know how to get Well by Fasting and Praying, for FREE! {See www.Amazon.com for: **"Did God or Satan Ordain Medical Doctors??" (Ask Huck Finn and/or Nigger Jim: because neither Tom Sawyer nor Judge Thatcher would Know!) By The Worldwide People's Revolution!®** Book 022, plus: **"The Complete SURVEYS of our VALUES!"** Book 059.}

12-18 [_] O Selected King, will it not be Extremely Stressful for Architects and Engineers to Design those Extremely Complicated Swanky Hotels, Castles, and Fortresses?

12-19 [_] Well, that is WHY all of the Chief Architects and Engineers must get Together, and Plan all such Things Carefully, According to the Desires of the People who are going to Live in them, who will likely Think of many Improvements, after Living within them for a few Years, whereby New Cities can be Improved, until they are Perfected.

12-20 [_] O Selected King, I Visualize a Million or more Different Ways to Build those Beautiful Planned City States, which would be Extremely Difficult to Redo, if they were done WRong.

(A List of the EVILS of CAPITALISM!)

— Chapter 13 —

Gambling with your Money or Life is Routine with Capitalists

13-01 [_] When a Capitalist goes into Business, there is no Guarantee that he or she will get any Customers at all, much less be Successful in Business: beCause it is a Dog-Eat-Dog Ordeal with so much Competition — such as the Restaurant Business, which is perhaps the Biggest Gamble you can take: beCause you have to Invest tens of thousands of Dollars in Equipment and Furniture, even before you can Open the Door and get one Customer! Therefore, if you do not have the Exact Right Location, and a Bunch of Repeat Customers, you are almost Guaranteed to go OUT of Business before you can get going: beCause there is often a lot of Expensive Foods that must be Dumped Out: beCause of Misjudging how many Customers MIGHT Happen to come in to Eat. After all, how can you Compete with Mega Companies, which Buy Truckloads of Foods at Greatly Reduced Prices, and Quadruple their Money on everything that they Sell? Therefore, that somewhat Explains HOW 10,000 or more People could get into the Restaurant Business, each Year, and 15,000 or more such Businesses go OUT of Business: beCause of Various Reasons; but, mostly beCause of Government Regulations, Taxes, Expensive Help, and Endless Bills to Pay. Indeed, if you have the "Right" Location, the Property Taxes, alone, can Eat Up all of your Profits, whereby you can become Depressed by it all, and even Suicidal. †‡

13-02 [_] However, at a Swanky Fortress, no such Situation could arise: beCause there would be no Property Taxes, and the Restaurant Equipment would be FREE, and Guaranteed for Life: beCause of being Designed to Endure for a thousand Years or more. After all, if there is a Need for such a Restaurant, the New RIGHTEOUS One-World GovernMINT will get you Set Up with it, and Properly so: beCause it is in their Interest to make everyone Prosperous and Happy, even if all such People must Attend Classes, whereby they can Learn HOW to be Successful, just by Following the RULES. Indeed, all of the Buildings, Houses, Cisterns, Gardens, and everything will Belong to that Good Government, until someone Earns and Saves enough Money to Buy it, if they Want to. However, there is no Need for any Person to Own any such Property, whereby they might be Gambling with their Money, when it is much more Practical for the Government to Produce those Good Things that are Needed for True Prosperity — such as Planting Billions of Fruit Trees: so that everyone can have all of the Fresh Natural Sweet Fruit Juices and Fruits that they might Want to Drink or Eat, at Cost, or even for Free, if you have Joined **"The Swanky Associations of Working Soldiers!" (A Fascinating Collection of Various Kinds of Voluntary Working Soldiers!) By The Worldwide People's Revolution!®** Book 018.

13-03 [_] So, O Master Twain, if the Federal Government OWNS ALL of the Building Materials, Lands, Houses, Workshops, Cisterns, Gardens, Vineyards, Orchards, Parks, Transportation, and EVERYTHING, including the Businesses, is that not COMMUNISM?

13-04 [_] NO! It is "Swangkeenomiks," and not Communism: beCause you will still be Welcome to get into any Free Enterprise Business that you Want to, and you will be Assisted by that Good Government to Succeed; but, only IF it is a Necessary Business — such as Tool Making, Clothes

Making, Furniture Making, Tile Making, or something that is Needed; but, NOT Beauty Parlors, Beer Halls, Barber Shops, Car Repair Shops, nor any other Trash Dumps: beCause those Things are NOT Needed for True Prosperity, which Begins with a Good House, Large Cisterns for Water Storage, a one-acre Garden, a Home-craft Workshop, Well-made Tools, and a Sales Shop, where you may Sell your Fine Hand-crafted Furniture, for Example, which might Require a whole Year, or more, just to make a really Beautiful Piece of Furniture as a Master Craftsman might Do, after going to School to Learn HOW to Do it Correctly. After all, the Days of Producing Capitalist TRASH for Sale must come to an END.

13-05 [_] So, O Elected King, it Sounds like **"The New RIGHTEOUS One-World Government"** will be the BOSS, huh? Yes, they will Control the Money Supply, and thus Decide WHO gets Hired and Fired, huh?

13-06 [_] Well, since we have MILLIONS of Swanky Fortresses to Build, being about 4 Miles in Diameter, and being Designed for about 10,000 People, maximum, that alone will keep all of us Busy for many Years to come; but, when we get Finished, almost everyone will be Living within a Beautiful Swanky PALACE, if they Want to. However, if they do not Want to, they are Welcome to Live with Coyotes, Foxes, Skunks, and Snakes, in Caves, in the Wilderness, or even within Abandoned Cities of Confusion: beCause they will be Free to do that.

13-07 [_] O Selected King, I had the Impression that we would Build just 2 or 3 Giant City States for everyone in the Country; but, now you say that we will be Building MILLIONS of Little City States! So, which Way is it?

13-08 [_] Well, that will have to be Decided after we Hold **"The GREAT Worldwide TELEVISED Court HEARING!"** Indeed, it could be that it is Impractical to Build such Giant Cities: beCause of not being Able to Manage them Properly without Creating Criminals. After all, not everyone is Civilized enough to Do that without Special Problems — such as Secret Gangs Forming, which would never be the Case within a Small Fortress, which would be Easy to Govern, and without any Police DEPARTment: beCause of the Simplicity of such a Lifestyle, which Fortress would consist mostly of Moderately Rich Gardeners, who would have their Palaces. In Fact, it could be that the Ideal Plan is to Build nothing but **"Beautiful Swanky PALACES!" (A New Concept in Living Habits — Swanky Palaces for Poor People!) By The Worldwide People's Revolution!®**, Book 066, which I have also Described in: **"The Environmentalists' Paradise!" (HOW almost Everyone could be Living in a Beautiful Manmade Paradise!)**, Book 035. Indeed, there are Advantages for doing that, even if those Palaces are Built Back-to-Back within Large Cities: beCause each Palace can have its own Elected King and Queen to Govern it, whereby the People can have more Freedoms, including their Beer Parlors, if they Want them. However, such a System would Require *"the Mark of the Beast"* just to Control them, which is a Numbering System, whereby each Person has his or her own Personal Permanent Positive Identification Numbers, whereby he or she cannot go anywhere, nor Buy nor Sell anything without his or her Numbers, whereas a Small Swanky Fortress would not Require any such Numbers: beCause everyone within the City would Know everyone else, and all of them would have Congressional Meetings, Church Services, and Communal Entertainments, much like a Big Family, which Lives in Peace. {See www.Amazon.com for **"LIGHTNING STRIKES Versus Lightning Bugs!" (HOW you can Become Moderately RICH, without Telling any Lies nor Selling any Trash!) By The Worldwide People's Revolution!®**, which gives a Concise

(A List of the EVILS of CAPITALISM!)

Description of **"The GREAT Worldwide TELEVISED Court HEARING,"** whereby all such Important Issues can be Discussed, and anyone may Contribute his or her Honest Opinions for us to Meditate on, whereby we might Decide what is Best for all of us. Indeed, I have already Proposed the Building of 7 Different Kinds of Swanky Fortresses, just to Accommodate Various Kinds of People; but, it could be that someone has a Better Plan, which we all Need to Hear about at **"The GREAT Worldwide TELEVISED Court HEARING!"** †‡ {See the Link below, for: **"FREEDUM uv SPEECH!" (A Special Magazine of Honest Opinions!)**, Book 030-0001.}

13-09 [_] O Selected King, if your Master Plan is a Revelation from GOD, there is no Way that we could Improve on it by any Means.

13-10 [_] Well, that is True. However, not everyone will be Satisfied with God's Master Plan, which People must be Proven to be at Fault by Means of Reason and Logic. For Example, many Americans would no doubt Argue that Capitalism is much Better than Swangkeenomiks: beCause it makes it Possible for Rich Hogs to get most of the Money, while the Masses of Billions of People must Suffer in their States of Extreme Poverty, unless they Play the Capitalist Game, which is to:

- A-[_] Go into Debt by tens of thousands of dollars to go to the School of Fools and get a so-called "good education" without a Capital G nor E, as in a Really GOOD Education, whereby one might become like Jesus Christ, Moses, Elijah, Paul, or someone with some BRAINS. {See www.Amazon.com for: **"The Public School of IGNERUNT FQLZ!" (HOW we have been GRAATLEE DISEEVD by Capitalism!)**, Book 024, plus: **"Are you a Jobless Graduate of the SKQL uv FQLZ?" (HOW to get a GOUD EJUKAASHUN without Robbing the Bank!) By The Worldwide People's Revolution!®** Book 020.}

- B-[_] Work Hard and Save your Money: so that you can Invest it in some Capitalist Business — such as that Failing Restaurant Business. (Remember that more than 2 Million of them went Out of Business during the Great Bankers' Depression of the 1930's, while Following the Capitalist Rules!) †§‡

- C-[_] Play by the Rules, and go to your Friendly Banker to Borrow enough Money to get into a Really GOOD Business — such as one of the 520,000 American Businesses that went OUT of Business during the Great Bankers' Recession of 2008—2009. †§‡

- D-[_] Trust your Loving Federal Government, which calls Failing Banks "receiverships." Yes, the FDIC (Federal Deposit Insurance Corporation) assures us that "all deposits are backed up by the full faith and credit of the United States Federal Government," which is only 22 Trillion Dollars in DEBT! How Comforting, huh? Indeed, each Person is Insured "up to 250,000$ for each deposit ownership category in each insured bank," whatever that Means. This is to Insure that Moderately Rich People do not Lose everything under 250,000$; but, certainly everything above that Amount, whereby a Person with 20,000,000$ in the Bank might Lose all but 250,000$! Very Comforting, huh? Yes, it is the Nature of Capitalism, whereby you can be Rich Today, and Broke Tomorrow: because the Property Tax, alone, might be 300,000$ on your Insecure Business. †§‡

E-[_] Invest your Extra Money in Stocks and Bonds: beCause they are Safe Investments — such as Enron and Worldcom. †§‡

F-[_] Buy a "good" house in a "good" community — such as in Detroit, Michigan, where half or more of the City packed up their Bags and DEPARTED! †§‡

G-[_] Pray to God when all else Fails: beCause he, alone, is Trustworthy and Reliable when the Atomic and Hydrogen Bombs are Dropping on your almost Empty Head. †§‡§§

H-[_] Homeland Security Agents will take Good Care of you, if you have been a Good Citizen, and have Paid your Taxes on Time — even as they took Good Care of Osama bin Laden, who used to Work for the CIA, who Died 10 Years before they Allegedly Killed him in Pakistan in 2011. (See YouTube Videos for the Proof.)

I-[_] Get your Wooden / Plastic Firetrap House INSURED at all Costs: beCause you will Abandon it when the Great False Economy CRASHES, which will Happen when the Masses of People come to Realize that they have been ROBBED, Lied to, RAPED, Deceived, and CASTRATED by Capitalism, whereby they are Impotent to Do anything about it — except to Abandon Ship — or, VOTE for The GOAT!

J-[_] Justice Demands that we BURN the Old Whore with FIRE for her Multitude of Sins and Lies: beCause it was Possible and much more Practical for everyone to be Living within Secure Swanky Fortresses, and with less Wasted Energy, Time, Money, and Materials! †§‡

K-[_] Kings and Kweenz will become Paupers, if they are not Wise, and Agree with **"The Swanky Sword of Divine Truths!"** Book 067.

L-[_] God will have the Last Laugh during the Judgment Day, when he will say: "Did I not Send to you my Selected King to be your Righteous King, and Help you to Truly Prosper and Live in Peace? But, you Chose to Prostitute yourselves to the Evil Empire for the Sake of Clinging to your Vain Traditions, which never Profited you anything: beCause you Traded your Good Health and True Wealth for the Vain Things of the World, which cannot Satisfy the Soul, while Depriving yourself of my Blessings. Therefore, Eat your Mud Pies and Drink your Recycled Sewage Water."

M-[_] And all of these Evils have come upon us for the Love of MONEY, which is **"The Root Cause for almost all Evils!" (The Strange Things that People Say and Do to Get more Money!) By The Worldwide People's Revolution!®** Book 078.

N-[_] Not everyone will Check the above Box, O Selected King: beCause they are still Persuaded within themselves that Capitalism will somehow Save them from the Great Famine that is Coming, when it does not Rain for 3 Years and 6 Months. †§‡ (See *Revelation 11,* King James Version.)

O-[_] Are there no OPTIONS, O Selected King? Can we not now Humble ourselves, and Confess the GOODNESS of those Glorious Swanky Fortresses, and thus get ourselves Prepared for the Worst Conditions? {See www.Amazon.com for: **"GLORIOUS Swanky**

(A List of the EVILS of CAPITALISM!)

Hotels Castles and Fortresses!" (Beautiful Planned City States for WISE Intelligent Well-Educated People with Common Sense and Good Understanding!) By The Worldwide People's Revolution!® Book 019.}

P-[_] Perhaps Americans will be Willing to Listen to Reason and Logic when their Bellybuttons are Rubbing on their Backbones for Hunger and Thirst in Siberian Prison Camps; but, I Doubt it: beCause they have been Sold Down the River into Slavery with Poor Nigger Jim, and Poor Ignorant Huck Finn is not Able to Rescue them. Yes, they are Prisoners of a Sick Society, which has its Priorities completely OUT of Order.

R-[_] Righteousness Requires a RIGHTEOUS One-World GovernMINT, which has an Unlimited Amount of New Money, which it Uses WISELY, in Order to HIRE whomever is Willing and Able to Learn and Work, in Order to Help Build those Beautiful Planned City States in Various Sizes, Shapes, and with Various Colors of Rocks, which will Represent that New Money, which will make it the very Best Money in all of the World: beCause it will have to be Earned by Honest Labor, without any Loans, without any Interest, and without any Taxes: beCause everyone LOVES such a Good GovernMint, whereby they Cheerfully Donate whatever Money is Required for Operating it.

S-[_] All of the Saints will Check the above R-Box: beCause they Agree with GOD.

T-[_] I Testify that whomever does not Check the above R-Box is Suspect of being an Anti-Christ Demon-possessed Capitalist, who should be Summoned to Court, and Forced to Prove what is WRong with it, or else be Stuffed into one of Adolf Hitler's Crematory Ovens: beCause only Lying Conniving Edomites will Disagree with it. †§‡

U-[_] I Understand that this is very Serious Literature, and the Punishment for the Rejection of all such Great Provable Truths is the Seven Last Great Plagues!

V-[_] The Victory is by FAITH, Hope, Trust, Love, Patience, Persistence and OBEDIENCE to the Truth. Therefore, I will Submit, and also Learn whatever Truths are Necessary to Save my Soul. {See www.Amazon.com for: **"God Speaks and the Whole World Listens!" (Fire on the Mountain from the Burning Bush by the Spirit of Truth!)**, Book 026, plus: **"DIETS!" (A Reasonable Solution for the "Eternal Controversy"!)**, Book 037, plus: **"FREEDOM uv SPEECH!" (A Special Magazine of Honest Opinions!) By The Worldwide People's Revolution!® Book 030-0001.}**

W-[_] Without Faith, it is Impossible to Please God, who will Permit Satan to Work Up another World War, if we do not Quickly Submit to **"The Swanky Sword of Divine Truths!" (The Most Powerful Weapon in the Whole Universe!)**, Book 067, and Cooperate with our Selected King before he Dies with a Broken Heart.

X-[_] X-amount of People are still Sold on the "Goodness of Capitalism," in spite of all of the Evidences Against it.

Y-[_] I am Yearning for the Day of Gladness when all Wars CEASE, and everyone is Living in PEACE. {See the above Link for: **"The Right Design for Living!" (A List of Great Advantages for Building Beautiful Planned City States!)**, Book 012.

Z-[_] I Agree, O Zebra; but, first, we need another Good Sermon to Inspire us.

— Chapter 14 —

A Good Sermon from the Master Farmer

14-01 [_] You People have had about 6,000 Years to Learn your Lessons, and to Experiment with your DUMBmocracy, Capitalism, Communism, Socialism, Fascism, and whatever — none of which was According to my Master Plan — and therefore, you have Proven yourselves to be Incapable of Governing yourselves in Peace: beCause of Rejecting **"The Seven Basic Spiritual Building Blocks of LIFE,"** as if you could Separate the Heart of the Body of Good Government from the Head, and still have a Functioning Body. Indeed, you have Experimented with "Countless" Religions and Political Beliefs; but, you have never Truly Tried to Love nor Obey all of my Commandments, much less the New MAGNIFIED Version of the 20 Commandments, which you can find in: **"LIGHTNING STRIKES Versus Lightning Bugs!" (HOW you can Become Moderately RICH, without Telling any Lies nor Selling any Trash!) By The Worldwide People's Revolution!®**, Book 074, which also contains a Special Chapter, called: **"WHO QUALIFIES to Rule Over US?"**

14-02 [_] Therefore, I have Stretched Out my Arms of Love and Compassion toward you People one Last Time, with the Hope that you might Listen to Reason and Logic, and thus Do what is RIIT and GOUD for yourselves; but, behold, I already Know in Advance how STUPID most of you are, which I can Judge by your Evil Works, whereby you call that which is Evil something Good, while calling that which is Good something Evil. For Example, rather than Confess the Evils of Making and Using those Stinking and Dangerous Cars, Vans, Pickups, Trucks, Buses, Tractors, Lawnmowers, Chainsaws, and many other Stinking Noisy Abominations, you Persist in Trying to Justify them, as if they were Necessary for True Prosperity. Indeed, I will Confess that Bulldozers and Trains are very Useful and Necessary Tools for True Prosperity: beCause they can be Used Wisely for Building those **"GLORIOUS Swanky Hotels Castles and Fortresses,"** which are Designed for True Prosperity, which Tools are Permissible to Use, as well as Rock-cutting and Rock-polishing Machines: beCause they are most Practical Mechanical Slaves, which will never Complain about Low Wages.

14-03 [_] However, when it comes to Good Health, and HOW to Obtain and Maintain it, you People have Completely Missed the Boat, you might say, and have Fallen into a Deep Dark Drug PIT, which will be most Difficult to Rescue you from: beCause a Deceived Person does not Realize that he or she is Deceived; but, such is the Case with most Americans and "Civilized" People, Worldwide, who have been Sold a Pack of Lies, who are now Addicted to Various Kinds of Drugs, which is rather Humiliating, I would Think; but, I am Sure that most of those Drug Addicts will not be Willing to Confess it, which is Okay with me: beCause I am not the Unholy One who is Suffering with any such Addictions. Indeed, I am Free, Healthy and Happy with a Capital F and H, while most of you Adults are nothing but SLAVES of one Kind or another — as in Education Slaves, Work Slaves, Tax Slaves, Insurance Slaves, Usury Slaves, Drug Slaves, and Endless Bills

(A List of the EVILS of CAPITALISM!)

Slaves — which is also Okay with me: beCause I Know for a Fact that if you Suffer Long Enough, you will come to your Right Senses with the Prodigal Son of *Luke 15* — that is, IF your Brains are Functioning well enough to Understand what is Happening, and especially when the Rain STOPS, and all of your Forests and Fields DRY UP and BURN UP, whereby you are left in a much Worse Condition than the Prodigal Son, who at least had a Home to Return to, and a Father who Loved him, while you People have Turned your Backs against me, and Refuse to even Consider that my Selected King is my Chief Servant: beCause he is most Honest, who has every Right to Believe as he Believes: beCause much of the *Holy Bible* is a Mutilated Book, which cannot be Trusted. However, there are also some very Plain and Easy-to-Understand Parts — such as that Story about the Prodigal Son, which almost everyone can Relate with: beCause of going Astray from the Path of Life, which Leads into the Blest Land of Perfect Oneness with God, who is All that is GOOD, who cannot Rightly be Blamed for the Evil Conditions in this World of Woes: beCause those are Doings of Satan, the Devil, even as you can read about **"In thu Beeginingz uv Thingz!" (Thu Kreeaashun Stooree frum thu Beegining!) By The Worldwide People's Revolution!®** Book 025. Yes, it also Requires Faith, Hope, Trust, Love, Patience, Persistence and Obedience, just to Plow through it; but, you will be Glad if you Do Plow through it: beCause it Unravels many Mysteries, even as **"Thu Nq MAGNUFIID Verzhun uv Thu PROVERBZ uv KING SOLUMUN in Plaan Innglish,"** Book 028, also Solves many Mysteries, and makes those Proverbs Plain and Understandable, which everyone should Study in the Quietness of a Peaceful Park, in a Comfortable Easy Chair, where the Little Birds of Cheerfulness are Singing, and the Ducks are Swimming in a Pond, and the Squirrels are Playing in the Trees. Yes, it is Good to be Connected with the Real World when Studying the Inspired Words of Provable Truths, and Especially when you are Reading **"The Gospel According to our Elected King!" (The Good News from the Most Modern Perspective!)**, Book 077, which contains the Sermon of Jonah to the People of Nineveh, which is one of the Best Sermons ever given, which Caused 120,000 People to Repent with True Repentance, whereby they were Saved from Destruction. {See: **"The New MAGNIFIED Version of the GOOD NEWS According to Saint LUKE!" (The Magnified Gospel of Luke in Plain English!) By The Worldwide People's Revolution!®** Book 061.}

14-04 [_] Now, I fully Realize that most of you do not Trust my Selected King, and for Various Reasons: beCause, "he is a little Tricky," you might say. However, his "Tricks" are all rather Harmless and Innocent: beCause he has no Evil Intentions, whatsoever. In Fact, he could Care Less about Ruling Over anyone, and would much Prefer that each Person should Learn to Govern him or herself. However, not even that would Obviate the Need for Establishing a New RIGHTEOUS One-World GovernMINT, which has an Unlimited Supply of Good Money, which must be Earned by Honest Labor, without any Loans, without any Usury, and without any Taxes. Indeed, you have never Heard of a Better Plan than that, which is Perfectly Fair for everyone, including the Edomite Bankers, who can Discover New Occupations: beCause the Person who does the most Physical Labor, and the Best Job, should be Paid the most, according to **"A List of FAIR Swanky Wages,"** whereby a Strong Young Man might Earn as much as 120$ per Hour for Placing Heavy Stones on a Wall, by Working Together with other Voluntary Working Soldiers: beCause Great Things can be Accomplished by Working Together, while almost nothing Good can be Accomplished by the Independent Jackass Method. Therefore, Learn what it Means to Work by United Effort for a Common Goal: beCause People were Designed to be Communal Creatures, who should Share their Labors for the Benefit of everyone, and Cheerfully so, which they would Naturally Do, if they were Healthy, Wealthy, and WISE. Yes, I Know that you have been Inspired by Capitalist Hogs to be Greedy and Selfish, whereby they have taken Advantage of your

Ignorance; but, it is not the Way of the Gods, who have One Mind, One Heart, One Opinion, One Understanding, and One Holy Goal, which is to make most of Mankind into the Godly Kind, while Satan has just the Opposite Goal. Yes, he would like for you People to be in Eternal Wars with each other; and therefore, he Inspired False Religions by the Dozens, including those Radical Muslims, whose Evil Works Prove beyond any Doubt that they have a False Religion, which is also True for Capitalists, Communists, Socialists, Fascists, and other False Economic Systems, which can be Proven to be Evil in a Courtroom, if anyone is Interested in it. I would say that most People are not Interested in it: beCause of Fearing that their False Religions and Economic Systems are also FALSE. Yes, they Fear that they might have to Change their Ways of Thinking and Living — as if they were now Living in **"Beautiful Swanky PALACES!" (A New Concept in Living Habits — Swanky Palaces for Poor People!) By The Worldwide People's Revolution!®** Book 066. Indeed, they are not even Willing to Learn what a Swanky Palace IS, much less go to Work to Help Build a Million of them for themselves: beCause they Vainly Imagine that my Selected King might Claim all of them for himself! Otherwise, they are Afraid that my Selected King might DIE, and that some Tyrannical One-World Government might make them into Slaves in Factories and Gardens — but, if not them, personally, then their Children! ‡

14-05 [_] Yes, their Fears are Unwarranted: beCause, once all of those **"GLORIOUS Swanky Hotels Castles and Fortresses"** are Finished, everyone in the World can Inherit them; but, NOT Own them as Personal Properties: beCause that is the Source of your Corruption. Indeed, you might Remember the Plan that I gave to Moses, and Instructed him to Divide the Land among all of the Children of Israel, among all 13 Tribes, which Joshua did, which was Wise of him, and which was Perfectly Fair, except that not all of that Land was Worth Inheriting, being Wasteland. Indeed, much of the World is Presently just a Wasteland, which could hardly Feed anyone, which must be Transformed in Productive Land by the United Effort of **"Seven Great Armies of Working Soldiers!" (HOW to Provide a Way for Everyone to WORK: so as to Eliminate Poverty, Crimes, Drug Abuses, Prisons and Unnecessary Taxes!) By The Worldwide People's Revolution!®**, Book 015: beCause that is Possible and most Practical, and without any Selfishness nor Greed. In Fact, it should be the Responsibility of those Israelis to take Charge and Help those Poor Palestinians to Build their own Swanky Fortresses, before the Israelis Build their own, and to do a Good Job of it: beCause they have the Technologies to do that. Likewise, it should be the Responsibility of the Big Chiefs in Washington, District of Criminals, to Build Beautiful Swanky Palaces for those Poor Indians, who should be Happy to Volunteer to Help: beCause it does not Require a LOT of Education to Mix Up Concrete for making Cisterns for Water Storage; but, it does Require Good Masters in Charge of it, which is where the Architects and Engineers will come in Handy, who can Plan all such Cities Properly, and make them to Endure for thousands of Years: beCause this is your Eternal Home, O Ignorant FOOLS. Likewise, all of those Poor Black and Brown People Need Good Houses, Workshops, Well-made Tools, and Gardens to Work in with Adam and Eve, you might say; and therefore, their Swanky Hotels and Fortresses should be Built FIRST: beCause they have been Abused and Misused Long Enough. And other than that, the Poor Refugees should be Assisted to Build their own Beautiful Planned City States within their own Countries, where they Want to Live in Peace, and Prosper Properly.

14-06 [_] Now, you might say, "O Master Farmer, suppose we Run Out of Rocks to Work with, how will we get Swanky Palaces Built for everyone in the World?" Well, that is WHY you must take an Inventory of all Building Materials, in Order to make Sure that you do not Waste any Good Stones: beCause there is no Good Reason for making 10-feet-thick Marble Walls, when one-half-

(A List of the EVILS of CAPITALISM!)

inch-thick Polished Marble Tiles work well for Tiling Ugly Gray Limestone Rocks, which are found in Abundance. Indeed, all of the Beautiful Marbles, Onyxes, and Granites should be Saved for Swanky Castles, which will be Built after all People who Want to, are Living within Beautiful Swanky Fortresses, which should be Built after all of the Hotels are Finished: so that the Workers can Live in the Hotels while Working on the Fortresses, which will Require a few Years to Finish, even if you go about it like going to War, which is HOW you should go about Doing it: beCause, at the Rate that you Ignorant Greedy Selfish Fools are Polluting your Good Earth, the Antarctic Ice is likely to MELT, along with Greenland's Ice, and thus Cause your Oceans to Rise by 20 Feet or more, whereby you will have a General Disaster on your Hands, Worldwide! Yes, Ask your Scientists, if you Doubt it: beCause, with Satan in Command, all such Evil Things can Happen! ‡

14-07 [_] Therefore, Do as I Command you, and you will be Healthy, Wealthy, and WISE. Yes, you will be Blest with Perfect Peace, and all Hateful Wars will CEASE: beCause of Faith, Hope, Trust, Love, Patience, Persistence, and OBEDIENCE! Yes, it is just that Simple and Beautiful. Therefore, be Wise, and Call for **"The GREAT Worldwide TELEVISED Court HEARING!" (That Great Meeting of the Most Intelligent and Well-Educated Minds!) By The Worldwide People's Revolution!®**, Book 041, lest I Smite the whole Earth with a SORE CURSE! Yes, some Ignorant Fools might even Think that it is FUNNY; but, I will have you Know that I still Control the Wind and the Rain, and can Intervene in Worldly Affairs, even as during Ancient Times: beCause Satan is Happy to Destroy you; but, I Want to Save you Alive, and Prosper you, and Bless you with Good Gifts. However, I am Unable to Do that without Following Divine LAWS, one of which Requires that all of you People REPENT, which is WHY that I Inspired my Selected King to write: **"The Gospel According to our Elected King,"** Book 077, which some of you might also Imagine is a JOKE of some Kind; but, when the Rain STOPS, it will be too Late to Repent: beCause there will be no Sweet Fruits to Break your Fasts on. Indeed, the Gross Grocery Stores will be EMPTY! Therefore, you can now Understand that Satan has you Caught in his Trap, which you Set for yourselves by Listening to his Sly Deceptions and Lies. Therefore, he is now Laughing at YOU, O Fools. Indeed, you do not even have a Pantry full of Stored Foods, much less GOOD Foods, nor several Half-Million-gallon Cisterns for Water Storage for each Family. In Fact, you Played right into his Hands, by Imagining that you should not take any Thoughts for Tomorrow, for what you shall Eat nor Drink, nor for how you shall be Clothed, as if you were my Chosen Disciples, when you are nothing but Ignorant FOOLS, which can easily be Proven in a Courtroom with Law and Order, with a Riichus Juj in Charge of it!

14-08 [_] Therefore, be Wise, before you are Eating your own Cats and Dogs: beCause of your Hunger: beCause Satan will also Kill your Livestock with Plagues, and leave you with nothing! Yes, all such Evil Things are Possible and most Practical for Correcting Rebels and Hardhearted Sinners, who would be Wise to REPENT, while it is most Practical and Possible. Otherwise, you will DIE, and then you will be Judged According to your Words and Works, whereupon you will be Assigned to the Perfect Place for you in a Lower Order of Worlds, where you can be Tormented both Day and Night, forever and ever, until you REPENT: beCause there is no other Way to be Saved from it. Therefore, do not be Fools, any longer, nor little Spiritual Babies, like President Donald Trumpeter and his Vice President, Mike Pence, who should be Ashamed of themselves for not Growing Up, who are still Nursing on the Tits of a Capitalist Goat, who would Destroy the Whole Earth for the Sake of the Great God GUT; but, you should be Wise, and Demand that Great Meeting of the Most Intelligent Minds, and Establish **"The New RIGHTEOUS One-World Government!" (HOW to Establish a Righteous One-World Government without Going to**

WAR!) By The Worldwide People's Revolution!®, Book 056, and then go to Work, Building **"The Great World TEMPLE of PEACE!" (The Glory of Jerusalem Arises Again!) By The Worldwide People's Revolution!®**, Book 017, which will be the Headquarters for that New Righteous One-World Government. Yes, the Glory of Jerusalem will Arise Again, if you make it so, and I will also Suddenly Return to be your Righteous King, even the KING of Kings and the RULER of Rulers! Amen.

14-09 [_] Now, I Hear someone, who is like a Frog, croak: "O Master Farmer, how can we Know for Sure that it is YOU who are Instructing us, and not some Pea-brain Peacock with a Great Tale of Outlandish LIES?" Well, O Frog, if you cannot Distinguish the Voice of the Master Farmer, by now, then you Deserve to Suffer through the Great Tribulation: beCause you are not Fit for any Position in the Holy Kingdom of All that is Good. Moreover, I Challenge you to Present any of those so-called "Outlandish LIES," which you Failed to Mention. Indeed, if my Selected King had made one hundredth as many False Promises as those Silly Powerless Politicians, I could Understand WHY you would be Unwilling to VOTE for The GOAT! {See www.Amazon.com for: **"Mark Twain Races for the PRESIDENCY!" (The 2020 Presidential Candidates Desperately Need Some STRONG Undefeatable COMPETITION!) By The Worldwide People's Revolution!® Book 033.**}

14-10 [_] Remember this, if you Do what I say, and you all end up Living in **"Beautiful Swanky PALACES"** with Peace and Happiness, you will be Glad you did, no matter what else might Happen; but, if you do not Do as I say, and the Rains STOP, you will be in Extreme Misery, which will be Hell on the Earth, and in all of its Satanic Glory! Therefore, come to your RIIT Senses, and Study my Master Plan for Worldwide Law, Order, Obedience, Peace and True Prosperity: beCause it is Possible and most Practical if almost all People are Moderately RICH. Indeed, there are some People who are Mentally Deficient or Defective, who could never be Rich in any Way: beCause they do not Recognize a Tree-ripened Peach from a Cactus Plant, and would not be Able to Describe the Difference between them. Therefore, just Forget about those Poor Pitiful People, and Concentrate on Helping the People who are Willing and Able to Help themselves, who are in Need of the 5,000-plus Advantages for Building and Living within the Borders of those **"GLORIOUS Swanky Hotels Castles and Fortresses!" (Beautiful Planned City States for WISE Intelligent Well-Educated People with Common Sense and Good Understanding!) By The Worldwide People's Revolution!®** Book 019. Indeed, one of the Greatest Advantages for those Beautiful Planned City States, is the Fact that IF you Discover some Outlaw or Rebel Child within your City State, and you cannot Manage to Correct him or her, you can simply BANISH that Person, and thus be Rid of the Problems that he or she might Cause. Yes, you may Throw that Person Out of the Doorway, even as you might now Throw a Rat Out of the House for a Cat to Eat, and it will not Bother my Conscience the Slightest Bit, even if that Person becomes Food for a Hungry Lion, Bear, or Pack of Wolves, who should be left to Live on the Outsides of those Swanky Fortresses, just to WARN those Rebels and Outlaws to not be Rebellious: beCause it is Possible to be Cursed for it. After all, there should be thousands of Different Kinds of Swanky Fortresses, whereby each Person can Discover Like-minded People to Live with, just by Filling Out and Filing **"The Complete SURVEYS of our VALUES!" (SURVEYS of Religious Spiritual Political Governmental Sexual Social Moral Economic Business Labor Habitual and Miscellaneous VALUES!) By The Worldwide People's Revolution!® Book 059.** Yes, that will Require a little Time and Patience, O Children; but, it will Solve hundreds of Potential Problems, if not Billions of them! Selah. Stop and THINK. Meditate on it. Amen.

(A List of the EVILS of CAPITALISM!)

— Chapter 15 —

The Conclusion

15-01 [_] Now, as you can See, I did not List nearly ALL of the Evils of Capitalism by any Means; but, I did give to you some Idea concerning WHY God Hates that Evil Economic System, which allows so many Billions of People to go on Suffering, needlessly: beCause the World certainly does not Lack any Natural Resources for making everyone Moderately Rich, if they Want to be. Indeed, those Greedy Red Jew Bankers can now Practice what Moses Taught in *Leviticus 25,* and just FORGIVE ALL DEBTS: beCause they have Sufficient Wealth to take Good Care of themselves for at least ten thousand Years — not that they are Worthy of it; but, that they have nothing to Complain about.

15-02 [_] O Selected King, I was Hoping that you would make a very LONG Boring List of the Evils of Capitalism, which would Require a Person to spend a Month or more Reading it, whereby we could make ourselves SICK of Capitalism. After all, there must be no less than 5,000 Evils that are Associated with Capitalism, Directly or Indirectly, which has Produced all of these Hateful Wars, Greedy Selfish Bankers, Corrupt Politicians, Unjust Judges, Deceptive Witchdoctors, Drug Pushers, Prison Builders, and a Host of Drug Addicts, who barely know their Left Hands from their Right Hands, who are Drunk on Drugs of Various Kinds, including Religious Drugs, whereby they are Addicted to False Doctrines.

15-03 [_] Well, if you Notice, I have left a couple of Pages at the End of this Book for your own Personal List of Evils concerning Capitalism, which you are Welcome to Present at: **"The GREAT Worldwide TELEVISED Court HEARING!"** or in the **"FREEDUM uv SPEECH" (U Speshoul Maguzeen uv Onist Upinyuns!)** Book 030-0002. Yes, you may bring this Book with you for a Reminder of those Evils, along with all 140 other Books by the Selected King of **The Worldwide People's Revolution!®**, each of which you should Identify as your own Personal Book by Placing your Name and Address in each Book, and Telephone Numbers, if you have a Telephone, just in case a Book gets Lost in the Crowd. Yes, it will be a Bit Burdensome to Pack all such Books with you; but, if you have Checked the Appropriate Boxes, it could be Proven that you are Qualified to be Elected into some Position of Authority in that New RIGHTEOUS One-World GovernMINT, which will Prove to be a Great Blessing for you: beCause not many People would be Willing to Do that. Therefore, Print your Full Name Clearly with INK in all Books, along with your Birthdate, just in case someone else might have the same Name. (You would be Wise to get a Special Rubber Stamp made up with all of your Information on it, in large Readable Letters and Numbers, including your E-mail Address.) Moreover, if you have a Name like Smith, Jones, or Johnson, it might be a Good Idea to put other Names of near Relatives in the Books for "Insurance." After all, just one little Check Mark (X) in a Correct Box could be "the KEY into the Kingdom," you might say. Therefore, THINK before you ACT, and Understand that you are Free to ~~CROSS OFF~~ or ~~CROSS OUT~~ any Words that might make a Statement Read Correctly, in your Favor. For Example, [_] I am a ~~Stupid~~ Republican. [_] I am ~~an Ignorant~~ Democrat. [_] I am an Independent Jackass with an Ax to Grind and Sharpen for going to War against those Dimwitcrats and Reprobates, who seem to not be Able to Understand that there are more than 2 or 3 Different Ways to Look at something, or Interpret what is Meant by a certain Expression of Speech. For

Example, there is the Possibility that both Judge Brett Michael Kavanaugh and Christine Margaret Blasey Ford were Testifying for the TRUTH to the Senators during Thursday, September 27th, 2018, according to the Best of their Memories. (See: C-SPAN TV on the Internet.) However, being an Alcoholic, and being Totally Drunk at the Time of the Sexual Aggression on Christine, according to her Testimony, some 36 Years ago, when she was Talking with God about it, Judge Brett Kavanaugh would not likely Remember the Incident Clearly, if at all: beCause he was just Playing a Game with his Friend, ~~David~~ Judge, and probably had no Real Intentions of Raping Christine; but, just wanted to have some Fun with her, as in Teasing her, which was a very Bad Decision, which arose from Bad Judgments, which Proved him to be Unqualified to be a Supreme Court Justice, even if the Remainder of his Life was without Spot nor Blemish: beCause he never Gave Up the Drinking, nor had a Real Change of Heart, as a True Christian might, who would become a New Creation in Christ, who was NOT an Habitual Drinker, who may have had 3 or 4 Alcoholic Drinks during his entire Life. However, if Judge Kavanaugh comes to a Public Court, and Confesses ALL of his Sins, which he could do in some Church, and Proves that he is now such a New Creation in Christ, who Wants to Do what is Riit for everyone, including himself, he could be Rightly Appointed to that Position as a Supreme Court Justice for 4 Years, as a Test of his Faith, whereby he might Prove himself to be Acceptable and Electable for 4 more Years; but, only IF he Grew a Beard, and Acted like a Sober Grown MAN, instead of a Spoiled Rich Man's Baby Boy. Otherwise, some other more Qualified Person should have that Position of Authority, in my Honest Opinion. After all, among 300-million or more People in **"The Divided States of United Lies!" (The so-called "United States of North America" in Disguise!)**, Book 058, there should be at least a Dozen Righteous MEN to Hold the Offices of Supreme Court Justices, along with a Dozen Righteous WOMBMEN, who should Remove the Paints from their Faces, and the Perfumes from their Buttockses, and Wear Modest Clothing, and at least ACT like Women should as Good Examples for all Young Ladies to Follow, as the Apostle Paul might say: beCause a Loudmouthed Disrespectful Overbearing WOman with Makeup, Paint and Stinking Perfume on her Butt is about the most Disgusting Creature on the Earth, being next to a Stinking SKUNK, who would be the Last Creature to Enter into the Holy Kingdom of All that is GOOD. Yes, she will do Well to be Humble, Meek, Teachable, Respectful, Honest, Quiet, Submissive, and Totally FEMININE: beCause that is the Way that her Creator God Wants her to be, whereby, if she Qualifies, she might be Born as a Man the next Time Around in the Recycling Process of Spirits. Otherwise, she is likely to be Born in some Jungle in Africa, where the Monkeys are Yacking, both Day and Night, along with a lot of Noisy Birds. †§‡

15-04 [_] O Selected King, are you Serious? I am not Able to Read 140 Books, much less Read each one 3 Times, just to make Sure that I have a Clear Understanding of your Master Plan. Indeed, Life is simply not Long Enough to Do that. And what is that Nonsense about the Inferiority of Wombmen — are you a Bigoted Misogynist. Would you have the Queen of England wearing a long Flowing Dress, like your Grandmother wore at her Wedding, down to her Ankles? Is that the Ladies' Fashion of the Future at all Swanky Fortresses? Moreover, will all of the Men be Wearing Modest Robes, like your own? †§‡ {See: **"The Gospel According to our Elected King!"** B-077.}

15-05 [_] Well, you will have Plenty of Time to Read Good Books when the Rain STOPS: beCause there will be nothing much else to Do but to Read Good Books. Indeed, when we March around Jericho 7 Times, and Sound the Trumpets, the Walls will Fall, and the Giant Corporations of the World will be left lying Low under their own Stones and Rubble Trash, you might say. Yes, Babylon or Confusion will Fall, and Great shall be the Fall thereof; but, out of the Ashes will Arise

(A List of the EVILS of CAPITALISM!)

a much Better Way to Live, in Peace and Harmony with each other and with the Whole Earth. {See: **"The END of CONFUSION!" (The Great CELEBRATION of the Magnificent Wedding of the Most Humble Honest Nations, and the Grand Year of JUBILEE!) By The Worldwide People's Revolution!® Book 050.**}

15-06 [_] O Selected King, are you Sure that it is not all just Wishful Thinking? After all, People do not like to Read Books, nowadays. Moreover, why did you not Answer those Important Questions — are you a Bigoted Misogynist, or what??

15-07 [_] Well, *some* People do not like to Read Books; but, other People just LOVE to Read Good Books, and they can Inspire the others to also Read them, if they will only be so Wise as to Pick Out Good Parts to Read to them, to Inspire them — such as the Sermon of the Master Farmer, and **"The Environmentalists' Paradise!" (HOW almost Everyone could be Living in a Beautiful Manmade Paradise!) By The Worldwide People's Revolution!® Book 035.** Remember that it was Capitalism that Caused many Lands to be Transformed into Deserts, including much of Afghanistan, Pakistan, Iraq, Iran, Turkey, Syria, Lebanon, Israel, Arabia, Egypt, Sudan, Ethiopia, Libya, Nigeria, Somalia, and much of China, India, Mongolia, and dozens of Countries around the World: beCause Capitalism Acts like the Nature of GOATS, itself, who will Eat the Fruits, Leaves, and the Bark of the Tree, itself, until they Kill it! However, the Tenderhearted Sheeps of the Good Shepherd are Contented to Eat the Fruits that Fall Out of the Trees, and the Grasses that Grow on the Ground under the Trees, and not Overgraze the Land: beCause of keeping themselves Spread Out over enough Territory to Manage it Properly, which is about one Acre per Family of SHEEPS, who are like the Disciples of Jesus Christ and their Followers. Moreover, I have nothing against Respectful Women, who are somewhat like my Mother and Grandmother, who set such Good Examples of True Women, who Avoided all Arguments, who Lived in Peace, and did their Duties as True Women. In Fact, if all Women in the Whole World were like them, there would be a whole lot less Problems in this World of Woes. ‡

15-08 [_] O Elected King of **"The New RIGHTEOUS One-World Government,"** when the Masses of People are Living in those **"Beautiful Swanky PALACES,"** most of that Political and Religious Nonsense will simply Disappear, and most People will become Humble Honest Gardeners and Workers in their Home-craft Workshops, making Beautiful Things for us to Richly Enjoy in our Swanky Palaces. ‡

15-09 [_] Well, that is also what I Visualize for the Future, except that I HOPE that all People will become much more Spiritually-minded, and will thus be Conversing with Holy Angels, after doing much Fasting and Praying. {See: **"HOW to Become a HOLY Man!" (40 Good Reasons WHY People Should FAST and PRAY!), Book 045,** which is a Companion Book of: **"The Proper RULES for FASTING!" (The Complete Instruction Manual for True Repentance!) By The Worldwide People's Revolution!® Book 046.**}

15-10 [_] O Elected King, I do Hope that you are Correct: beCause this Capitalist Madness has gone on Long Enough in the Production of TRASH; and it is all about Personal Ownership of Properties, which has Inspired the Lust for more and more Money, which is not even Needed for True Prosperity: beCause it is Possible and most Practical if we all SHARE our Mountains of Rocks, Minerals, Metals, and whatever we have in this World of Wonders to Work with, whereby we can Build those **"Beautiful Swanky PALACES"** for everyone, and all Live like Kings and

Queens in First Class PALACES, who Eat at **Royal Swanky Buffets!** Yes, you have Outlined it all in your Wonderful Books, which is MAGNIFIED in: **"The New MAGNIFIED Version of the Book of ACTS!" (The Understandable Version of the ACTS of the Apostles in Plain English!) By The Worldwide People's Revolution!**®, Book 063, which everyone in the Whole World should Study, Carefully, even if they cannot Manage to Read any other Book on this Earth! Yes, it is a most Marvelous Book, which I Love!

(A List of the EVILS of CAPITALISM!)

A Short Photo Gallery for Capitalism

{It is said that a single Picture is worth a thousand Words, which is only True if you can See Clearly, and Understand what you are Looking at. For Example, how many People in this World of Wonders have any Idea what the Nature of a Goat is? One would almost have to Live with Goats for several Years, just to get Well-Acquainted with them. Each one has a Different Nature, being very much like Capitalists, who get into Businesses of Various Kinds. However, Basically-speaking, Goats are Lovable Creatures, just like most Capitalists; but, some are rather Mean and Selfish, and like to Bully the other Goats. You could talk with Donald Trumpeter about that, and Ask him WHY? Like the Goats, I am Sure that he would have something to Blat Out at you — such as, "It is just my Nature. How can I Help it? I am a Big Bully, and that's Okay. Do you Envy me for my Successes in Life?" — to which you might Respond, "No, I do not Envy you; but, I do Pity you: because it is more Blest to Give, than to Receive." — to which he might Respond: "I Give a lot more than you might Imagine, and I am Happy with myself." — to which you might Respond, "If you are so Happy with yourself, why is your Belly so Big? Do you not Know that People who Overeat are Unhappy with themselves, and are Attempting to get Happiness from Eating or Drinking, whereby they are never Satisfied?" — to which he might Respond, "I would not Know for Sure about that, since I seldom Overeat and never Drink any Alcoholic Beverages. Indeed, I am a Man of Great Moderation, if you Notice: because I do not Weigh 200 nor 300 Pounds too much." — to which God might Reply, "But, you do Weigh much more than one of those Healthy Happy Goats, who can Leap right over your Head by 6 feet or more, and not even Brag about it, nor Expect any Gold Medals for doing it. Therefore, you will do Well to be more like a Sheep, who is Contented with Food and Clothing. After all, what will it Profit a Man, if he should Gain the Whole World, and Lose his own Soul for the Sake of Gaining more Wealth? Just Remember that no Liars nor Hypocritters will Enter into my Holy Government, with or without any Gold-plated Toilets."}

{The above Photo shows the Dome of a certain Church, which was Severely Cracked by a Bad Earthquake; but, it did not Fall Down, in spite of being up 50 feet from the Floor of the Church, and in spite of being some 400 Years Old. In other Words, the Dome was still Strong enough to Resist the Earthquake, while straight walls not far away were not Strong enough; and several of those Walls Fell Down. Fortunately, no one was Hurt by any of it. So, the Great Question is, "HOW can we Build SECURE Stone Dome Homes that will not be Affected by any Earthquakes, at all?" Well, the "Secret Solution" is to make Solid Concrete Domes about 10 feet THICK, and Cover them with 20 feet of Sand, Rocks, Gravel, Sand, Rocks, Clay, Sand, and Topsoil about 3 feet Deep, whereby the Rainwater can Drain into large Cisterns below the Dome Homes: beCause all Roofs should be Covered with All-Mineral Organic Gardens for the People who Live within them, who can walk straight out of their Front Doorways into their Gardens, which need to be about 3 to 4 feet below the Floor Levels of their Houses, just in case a Flood of Water should happen to come along. However, all of the Stone Dome Homes should be Built Up on TOP of Large Cisterns for Water Storage, whereby the Flood-plain is at least 50 feet below the Houses, and especially along Rivers, Lakes, Seas, and Oceans. In other Words, it calls for the

(A List of the EVILS of CAPITALISM!)

Construction of those **"GLORIOUS Swanky Hotels Castles and Fortresses!" (Beautiful Planned City States for WISE Intelligent Well-Educated People with Common Sense and Good Understanding!) By The Worldwide People's Revolution!®** Book 019.}

{Now, she may not be the Prettiest Girl in the World; but, she does have Natural Beauty, without any Makeup, Paint, Lipstick, nor Perfumes, which makes her Special in the Eyes of the Gods, who Love Natural Beauty, even as we all should. Her Eyes are especially Beautiful, being somewhat like the Light-brown Eyes of some of those Goats. However, many Women in this World of Woes are not Contented with their Natural Beauty: beCause they have been Bombarded with Hollywood Movies, which show the most Beautiful People that they can Discover, which Causes People with less Good Looks to Feel Inferior in some Ways, even though they should not pay any Attention to it: beCause God Judges us by what is Found in our Hearts or Innermost True Selves, who may be Good or Bad, Depending on what we Think and Meditate on, as well as the Kind of Company that we Keep, who could have Riches Untold: beCause of Keeping Company with Good Books, whereby we can have the Precious Gemstones of Truths and Wisdom in our Hearts. I did not get to Talk to her very much; and therefore, I have no Idea what might have been in her Heart; but, I Thanked her for being Natural and True to herself, and not some Painted Clown with a False Smile. I would say that she is just another Innocent Mexican, who has no Evil Desires to Sit on Gold-plated Toilets, while all around her are Hordes of Extremely Poor People.}

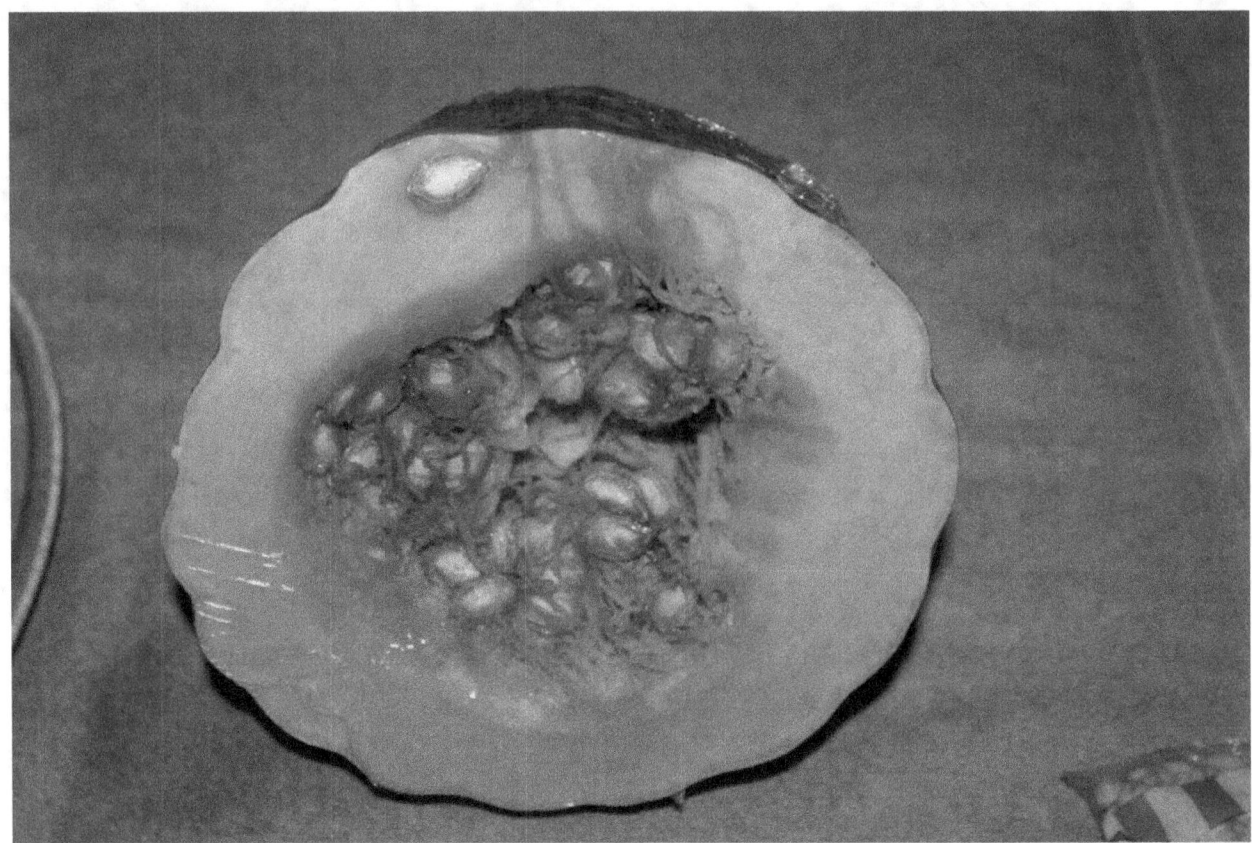

{The above Photo shows a Cut-open Squash, whereby you can See the Multitude of Seeds within it. Probably more than 100 Seeds. (The other half had just as many or more Seeds.) Now, just Stop and Think about that for awhile. Upwards of a Million People DIE during just ONE Day, on Average, in this World of Woes — all for the Lack of some GOOD FOODS, such as that Sweet Squash, which was just one on a Long Vine, which had about 10 of them, which took less than 5 Minutes to Plant 40 of them in a Corn Patch, which made similar Vines, which Produced more than 400 Squashes with the Richest of Flavors. (The Photo does not Show any of the Flavors.) Each Squash had its own Unique Flavor: beCause of being Fertilized with Various Kinds of Manures from Horses, Burros, Goats, Sheeps, Cows, Chickens, Turkeys, Ducks, Geese, and Peacocks! Yes, most People would not Know that each Animal has a Different Kind of Dung, which puts Different Kinds of Wonderful Flavors into Fruits and Vegetables, and especially when the Topsoil has Various Kinds of Powdered Rocks in it, which have been Digested in the Bellies of those Little Brown Earthworms, which are a Gardener's Favor Pets, you might say: beCause they do all of the Plowing, and Build up what is called "Soil Structure," whereby they make Tunnels for Tree Roots and other Roots to Follow, which Roots Gather up Minerals and Nitrogen for their Fruits and Nuts, which is a Marvelous Thing to Study, if you can Find the Time in the Capitalist World to Do that. Most People cannot Find the Time: beCause they are far too Busy Trying to get some Money to Pay all of their Endless BILLS, which is a Great Shame on them: beCause of being Deprived of the Better Things in Life, beginning with those Fruit Trees from the Garden of Eden, "if ye knows what I Means," as Huck Finn might say to Tom Sawyer during a Dark Cold Winter Night, when a Baked Squash like that might be the single Best Thing such a Poor Hungry Soul ever Ate!}

(A List of the EVILS of CAPITALISM!)

{Millions of Tourists go on Vacations every Year, and a Majority of them go to Places like Mexico, to see the Ancient Ruins of the Maya Indians, who did Amazing Construction Jobs.}

The Nature of CAPITALISM!

{That is your Selected King standing in front of the Pyramid of the Moon, about 20 Miles just Outside of Mexico City. I have on my Red Belt (Pocket), and White Robe with Green Trimmings, which are the Colors of the Mexican Flag. (Some Mexicans call me Santa Claus for Wearing the Robe.) I actually climbed up the Pyramid to get a Better View; and this is what I saw:}

{Off in the Distance, about a quarter of a Mile away, is the Pyramid of the Sun, which has a larger Base than the Great Pyramid of Egypt, which Base cannot be Seen in the above Photo: beCause it is behind other Structures. Nevertheless, you can Accept my Words for it — that it Required a HUGE Amount of Difficult WORK! Moreover, all of the Rocks in the dozens of other Structures at this Site, and at other similar Sites in Mexico, far Outnumber the Rocks that were used to Build the Great Pyramids of Egypt, as well as the Pyramid of the Sun: beCause they are no little Afternoon Projects in someone's Backyard. Furthermore, all of those Structures were done without any Payday, and NOT by any Slaves: beCause it was all Voluntary Work. In Fact, if you did not Like such Work, there was lots of other Necessary Work — such as Growing Fruits and Vegetables in Community Gardens, Washing Clothes, Cooking Foods, Grinding Corn, or whatever you Felt like Doing: beCause no one was in a Hurry to get Pyramids Built; but, it was like a Pass-time Project for Young People who Liked to Build Up their Beautiful Muscles, which almost all of the Boys and Young Men Liked to Do: beCause it made them Feel Good about themselves. Indeed, it was all Self-Rewarding Work, and a Great Pleasure to look back at it, at the End of the Day, and SEE whatever you Accomplished, which is not Possible with Cooking Meals, Hoeing Weeds in a Garden, nor Washing Clothes. Therefore, the Majority of the People Preferred to Work with the Rocks: beCause they could See what they Accomplished by

(A List of the EVILS of CAPITALISM!)

United Effort, which made them Feel like they were Needed and Wanted and Respected for it. After all, when you make a Beautiful Thing that is as Permanent as a Stone Pyramid, you are Really Living in a Construction Paradise — that is, when you are Building one of those **"GLORIOUS Swanky Hotels Castles and Fortresses,"** which are not just Beautiful; but, they are GLORIOUSLY Beautiful, and Wonderfully USEFUL! Yes, they are MAGNIFICENT Structures of the Highest Satisfactions: beCause you get to LIVE within them, and Enjoy all of the Marvelous Things that Witty People can Invent, and without going to the Moon!}

{There is another Marvelous Pyramid at Uxmal, which is pronounced Qsh-mawl, which must have taken many Years to Construct it, and it actually had a Service: beCause the Elected King could get up at the Top of it, and give a Speech to all of the People down below, who might have amounted to as many as 100,000 or more People, depending on what was Happening. Meanwhile, he could wait in the little Room for the Crowd to Gather, while Colorful Working Soldiers were arranging themselves on the Steps for a Special Concert, who wore very Decorative Costumes with Colored Feathers, Bells, and Ornaments on their otherwise mostly Naked Bodies, who had the Finest of Smooth Skins: beCause they had Perfected their Diets, which had no Refined Sugars, Cokes, nor Candies; but, they did have Sweet Fruits, Nuts, and Grains, among many Kinds of Vegetables, including Squashes, Tomatoes, Potatoes, Melons, Corns, Chili Peppers, and Green Leaves. Indeed, they all Ate like Royalties, every Day: beCause X-amount of them Volunteered to Fix the Foods for the others, who might be Working with the Rocks, or Thatching Roofs, or Packing Water from Pipes that Ran with Water all of the Time: beCause none of them figured out HOW to make Shut-off Valves; but, it did not matter: beCause none of the Water was Wasted: beCause it was Captured in Cisterns, which was used for Bathing, Washing Clothes, Cooking and Watering Gardens. Indeed, the whole System was

Organized by the Elders in the Community, who were Highly Respected by all of the People: beCause they had the most Education, the Better Skills, and Tools that were Needed for Working. Indeed, they were the Elite Class among the People, who were not Envied by the Lower Classes: beCause they all got to Eat at the same Tables, and could Enjoy their Smooth Skins just as much as any Elite Person might, who might even Envy them for their Beauty: beCause Hard Work makes Young Men much more Beautiful and thus Lovable. (See the next Page.) Therefore, it is Time to Stop and Enjoy some Pretty Clouds, which are Free of Charges.}

{Very few Americans have Time to Stop and Enjoy the Clouds: beCause they Live in their little Prison Cells, you might say, and especially if they Live in some very UGLY Place like New Yuck City, where there are only Glimpses of the Sky: beCause of being Blocked Out by those Tall Skyscrapers. Therefore, when would they get to See a Panoramic View of the Sky, like I can See from my own Garden on the Roof of my own House, at any Time I Look UP! Yes, I can also See the Mountains that Surround us on all Sides from 5 to 10 Miles away, which Remind me of those **"Beautiful Swanky PALACES!" (A New Concept in Living Habits — Swanky Palaces for Poor People!) By The Worldwide People's Revolution!**® Book 066. Yes, they will all be in Great TERRACES, with Fruit and Nut Trees Planted in all of the Terraces, along with Flower Gardens, Vegetable Gardens, Berry Bushes, Grape Vines, and Water Fountain — much like the Best of Scenery in Europe, except much more GRAND: beCause of the Tall Stone Terrace Walls with Arcades of Stone Wind Generators at the Tops of all of the Walls: so that everyone can have Free Electricity: beCause of Agreeing to WORK for it, while Feasting at **Royal Swanky Buffets!** Yes, what a Small Sacrifice, to Work for only 4 Hours of Common Skilled Labor per Day, or the Equivalent thereof, in Exchange for Living in a Beautiful Swanky Palace: beCause of

(A List of the EVILS of CAPITALISM!)

taking Advantage of those Mechanical Slaves, which will be Equally as Happy to Provide their Services for FREE, and without going on Strike for Higher Wages. Yes, it is the ONLY Rational Way to get it all Done without Wasting any Time Playing around with Worthless Money, which will be Meaningless to those **"Seven Great Armies of Working Soldiers!" (HOW to Provide a Way for Everyone to WORK: so as to Eliminate Poverty, Crimes, Drug Abuses, Prisons and Unnecessary Taxes!) By The Worldwide People's Revolution!® Book 015.**}

{That Avocado Potato Salad with Swanky Dill Pickles is as Good Tasting as anything you might Discover anywhere around the Trump Tower in New York City, in spite of Costing only 10 Dollars, which has Fresh Green Peas, Sweet Corn, Onions, Olives, Shredded Carrots, Lettuce, Celery, and other Goodies. That would be just one of a thousand Delicious Dishes at a **Royal Swanky Buffet!** Indeed, you cannot begin to Imagine what you are Missing: beCause of your EXTREME POVERTY! However, you might Rightfully Ask: "Just HOW could anyone Afford it, seeing that it would Require so much WORK to Grow and Harvest and Prepare all such Foods?" Well, I can Dig Up no less than 40 Bushels of Potatoes in less than 4 Hours, by Hand, which would be enough to Feed 500 People such a Salad, if you should Gather up 40 Bushels of Sweet Ripe Red Bell Peppers during the same 4 Hours, while Tim, Tom, Susan, Carol, and Jim Gather up their 40 Bushels of Sweet Corn, Peas, Tomatoes, and whatever else is Ready to Eat! Indeed, some Things — such as the Avocados and Ginger, might have to be Imported; but, by the United Effort of **"The Swanky Associations of Working Soldiers!" (A Fascinating Collection of Various Kinds of Voluntary Working Soldiers!) By The Worldwide People's Revolution!®**, Book 018, it is Possible for everyone to become Moderately RICH! Guaranteed! Indeed, Lazy Worthless People would be Sent to **"The Swanky Fasting Sanitarium,"** whereby they could get Regenerated — that is, unless they just Voluntarily Sent themselves over there, whereby they would be Rewarded for it. Otherwise, they could be Banished for their Craziness; and then they might find themselves Living in the Subways or Sewage Systems of New Yuck City, Lost Angels, Californicate, or in Highway Culverts around Lost Wages, Nevada. But, for Sure, no Sane Person would ever be Poor again, much less have any Needless Bills to Pay, nor any Needless Taxes: beCause those are Evil Fruits of CAPITALISM, not Swangkeenomiks.}

(A List of the EVILS of CAPITALISM!)

{The above Photo shows a Part of the Concrete Jungle of New York City, which some People say is "Beautiful." However, I Fail to See any Beauty in it: beCause it Looks like a Giant TRASH DUMP to me, and I Serious Doubt that Jesus Christ would Choose to Live there. But, Millions of People do Live there, and some even Like it! However, I would say that it is beCause they have never Seen any Beautiful Swanky Fortresses in all of their Naked Glory!"

The Nature of CAPITALISM!

{The above Photos shows the Entrance to the Chrysler Building in New York City, which is really Beautiful; but, you cannot See the Beauty of it in a Black and White Photograph, which is Exactly HOW an Unbeliever Views a Swanky Fortress in his or her own Mind, whereby the Unbeliever cannot Visualize what I am even Speaking of: beCause of having Eyes that cannot See Visions, and Ears that cannot Hear Truths. But, if you Want to get a Glimpse of a Swanky Fortress, just Visit the Chrysler Building in NYC.}

(A List of the EVILS of CAPITALISM!)

A Long List of other Fascinating Literature by the same Inspired Author

[_] 40-01 — **"LIGHTNING Versus the Lightning Bug!" (HOW almost Everyone can become Moderately RICH, without Telling Any Lies nor Selling Any Trash!)** Book 001.

[_] 40-02 — **"What is WRong with those Professing Christians?" (A Self-Examination of the Heart of the Body of Good Government!)** Book 002.

[_] 40-03 — **"For the Love of Money!" (The Strange Things that People Say and Do to Get more Money!)** Book 003.

[_] 40-04 — **"HOW to Prepare for CLIMATE CHANGES!" (The Wisest Plan for Mankind to Follow!)** Book 004.

[_] 40-05 — **"Why do I have to be Surrounded by CRAZY PEOPLE!" (Do almost all People Feel like they are Surrounded by CRAZY People??)** Book 005.

[_] 40-06 — **"The Washington Journal is a FARCE! (C-SPAN Managers are not very WISE!)** Book 006. (This Book has lots of Good Humor.)

[_] 40-07 — **"The PRAYERS of PUMPKINHEADS!" (Even God Needs a Little Humor to Cheer himself Up!)** Book 007. (Some of it is for Adults only.)

[_] 40-08 — **"A Sound Argument for Masters and Servants!" (WHY Everyone Needs a Good Master, and every Master Needs Good Obedient Servants!)** Book 008.

[_] 40-09 — **"WHY are some Preachers so POOR?" (HOW almost all Preachers could Get Moderately RICH, without Preaching any Outlandish LIES!)** Book 009.

[_] 40-10 — **"GOOD NEWS for REBEL WOMEN!" (HOW almost all Wives can become Moderately RICH without Leaving their Homes! Guaranteed!)** Book 010.

[_] 40-11 — **"The Low Court of Supreme Injustices is Brought to Trial!" (The Worldwide People's Revolution!® Butts Heads with the United States Supreme Court, with or without their Black Robes of Hypocrisies and Lies!)** Book 011. (This Inspired Book contains the Famous *Declaration of Interdependence,* which is a Must Read. It also contains the Correct Wording for the Placard on the Statue of Liberty.)

[_] 40-12 — **"The Right Design for Living!" (A List of Great Advantages for Building Beautiful Planned City States!)** Book 012. (This Book contains many Important Drawings, as well as HOW to Save hundreds of Trillions of Dollars by Building Swanky Fortresses, and Living in Peace within them. It is a Companion Book of Book 011, which contains many more Great Advantages for Fortresses.)

The Nature of CAPITALISM!

[_] 40-13 — "The Gospel According to The Worldwide People's Revolution!®" (The Good News from the Most Modern Perspective!) Book 013. (This Book contains the Famous Sermon of Jonah to the Ninevites, whereby 120,000 People Repented in Sackcloth and Ashes! Do not Miss Out on it.)

[_] 40-14 — "Poverty Hunger Riots Strikes Brutalities Election Deceptions and Civil Wars!" (The High Price that we Earthlings have Paid for Leaving the Good Land!) Book 014.

[_] 40-15 — "Seven Great Armies of Working Soldiers!" (HOW to Provide a Way for Everyone to WORK: so as to Eliminate Poverty, Crimes, Drug Abuses, Prisons and Unnecessary Taxes!) Book 015. (This Book contains a True Life Story when I was in the Army.)

[_] 40-16 — "The CONSTITUTION for the New RIGHTEOUS One-World GovernMint!" (HOW all Peoples can get True Justice, and Celebrate the Great Year of JUBILEE!) Book 016.

[_] 40-17 — "The Great World TEMPLE of PEACE!" (The Glory of Jerusalem Arises Again!) By The Worldwide People's Revolution!® Book 017.

[_] 40-18 — "The Swanky Associations of Working Soldiers!" (A Fascinating Collection of Various Kinds of Voluntary Working Soldiers!) Book 018. (There will be thousands of Associations for all Kinds of Occupations, which will Specialize in Fine Arts — such as Hand-carved Leather-bound Books. See "LIGHTNING STRIKES Versus Lightning Bugs!" Book 074, for a Good Example.)

[_] 40-19 — "GLORIOUS Swanky Hotels Castles and Fortresses!" (Beautiful Planned City States for WISE Intelligent Well-Educated People with Common Sense and Good Understanding!) Book 019. (This Book contains many Rough Drawings, which could be Greatly Improved upon by someone who Knows the Art, and has the Correct Computer Programs for doing it.)

[_] 40-20 — "Are you a Jobless Graduate of the SKQL uv FQLZ?" (HOW to Get a GOUD EJUKAASHUN without Robbing the Bank!) Book 020. (This Inspired Book contains the New MAGNIFIED Version {NMV} of *First Corinthians 13*, plus: HOW to Produce Pure Living Water!)

[_] 40-21 — "The LUSCIOUS All-Mineral Organic Method of Gardening!" (HOW to Grow DELICIOUS Satisfying Foods for Potential Kingz and Kweenz in Beautiful Swanky PALACES!) Book 021. (This Book Explains HOW to make a Flood-proof Garden, while Trapping the Rainwater.)

[_] 40-22 — "Did God or Satan Ordain Medical Doctors?" (Ask Huck Finn and/or Nigger Jim: because neither Tom Sawyer nor Judge Thatcher would Know!) Book 022. (This Inspired Book Reveals HOW to Prevent Common Colds, and has a Special Chapter that Explains what a True "Nigger" IS. Surprise yourself!)

(A List of the EVILS of CAPITALISM!)

[_] 40-23 — "The BIG White OUTHOUSE on the Not-so-Biblical Capitol DUNGHILL!" (The Chief Sins of the Divided States of United Lies!) By The Worldwide People's Revolution!® Book 023. (This Book contains Special Words that most People have never Heard! Surprise yourself again!)

[_] 40-24 — "The Public School of IGNERUNT FQLZ!" (HOW we have been GRAATLEE DISEEVD by Capitalism!) Book 024. (This Book Teaches Children HOW to "Reed and Riit in Funetik Ingglish in just wun Daa!" You should Challenge your Frendz and Naaberz with it.)

[_] 40-25 — "In thu Beeginingz uv Thingz!" (Thu Kreeaashun Stooree frum thu Beegining!) Book 025. {The Cover Photo shows a Picture of a Golden Supootaa (Sapote), which not one Person in a Million has ever Tasted: because it does not Ship very well, in spite of it being one of the most Sweetest Pleasant Fruits known to Mankind, which must Ripen on the Tree to be Extremely Good, after it is Grown Properly by "The LUSCIOUS All-Mineral Organic Method of Gardening!" Book 021, which Means that the Topsoil must have all of the Proper Minerals in it. Remember the Grapes of Eschol, which the Children of Israel brought back from the Promised Land in the *Book of Joshua,* which Required 2 Strong Men to Carry just one Cluster! See the Fascinating Photos in: "Orgimmick Gardening at its Best!" (HOW to Grow Delicious Satisfying Foods without a 10-Million-Dollar Investment!) By The Worldwide People's Revolution!® Book 079.}

[_] 40-26 — "God Speaks and the Whole World Listens!" (Fire on the Mountain from the Burning Bush by the Spirit of Truths!) Book 026. (This Powerful Book contains the Best Noah Story of all of the Books, including that of Gilgamesh the Great of Ancient Babylon!)

[_] 40-27 — "Does a Good Soldier have to be a MURDERER?" (Seven Great Swanky Armies of Voluntary Working Soldiers!) By The Worldwide People's Revolution!® Book 027. (Chapter 03 contains a True Life Story about a Dog Pile, which happened to me when I was just 10 Years Old.)

[_] 40-28 — "Thu Nq MAGNUFIID Verzhun uv Thu PROVERBZ uv KING SOLUMUN in Plaan Ingglish!" (The Understandable Version of the Famous Proverbs of King Solomon in Plain English!) Book 028. (This Marvelous Book MAGNIFIES each Proverb unto the Glory of the Great God of Inspiration, which is taken from the Original 4,000-page Book, which was written in less than 2 Months by the GIFT of Inspiration, which also contains the Famous Proverbs of Queen Izubelu!)

[_] 40-29 — "UNLIMITED ENERJEE 99 Percent Pollutions Free!" (HOW to Obtain FREE ElecTrickery, Worldwide!) By The Worldwide People's Revolution!® Book 029. (This Book contains the Jackson Brower Suicide, among many other Fascinating Subjects.)

[_] 40-30 — "FREEDUM uv SPEECH!" (U Speshoul Maguzeen uv Onist Upinyunz!) Book 030-0001, which contains the Great Advantages for Using Swanky Mulching Rocks in an All-Mineral Organic Garden, plus Baptism by Fire and Speaking in Foreign Languages! It is a Must Read. The Cover Photo shows a Portion of the Author's Marbleous Indian Countertop or Food Bar, which is just one Example of what you can also have in your own "Beautiful Swanky PALACES!" if you have the Honesty, Faith, Hope, Trust, Love, Patience, Persistence,

Cooperation and OBEDIENCE that are Required for True Prosperity! Therefore, Ejukaat yourself, and you will be Glad that you did!

[_] 40-31 — **"A Sure Cure for GUN VIOLENCE!"** (HOW TO STOP GANG WARS and CRIMINAL SHOOTINGS!) By The Worldwide People's Revolution!® Book 031. {The Cover Photo shows a Picture of a Short Shotgun, which is Fully Loaded with Double 00 Shells, and is Ready for any Tax Master who might Attempt to Steal the Retirement Home, who never moved a Finger to Help Build the Rock Houses, whereby we moved more than 66,666,666 Pounds by Hand, whose Property was Cunningly Stolen by that False Anti-Christ WICKED Cover-up Government, which allowed Bankers to Rob us of 30 Years of Hard Labor and more than 300,000 dollars-worth of Investments in our Uncommon American Farm, which is Explained in: **"LIGHTNING STRIKES Versus Lightning Bugs!"** (HOW you can Become Moderately RICH, without Telling any Lies nor Selling any Trash!) By The Worldwide People's Revolution!® Book 074, which contains many Photographs with Profound Explanations! Do not be left out in the Darkness of Ignorance. Get Informed, now: beCause, **"The Great False Economy is now DEBUNKED!"** Book 053.}

[_] 40-32 — **"AIIRMWVC and Reasonable Solutions!"** (Aliens, Illegal Immigrants, Refugees, Migrant Workers and other Victims of Capitalism!) By The Worldwide People's Revolution!® Book 032. (This Inspired Book contains *the New MAGNIFIED Version of Job 33*.)

[_] 40-33 — **"Mark Twain Races for the PRESIDENCY!"** (The 2020 Presidential Candidates Desperately Need Some STRONG Undefeatable COMPETITION!) By The Worldwide People's Revolution!® Book 033. {This Book contains a Part of my Autobiography, and my Personal Answers to the Questions in **"The Complete SURVEYS of our VALUES!"** (SURVEYS of Religious Spiritual Political Governmental Sexual Social Moral Economic Business Labor Habitual and Miscellaneous VALUES!) Book 059. It also contains many Black and White Photographs.}

[_] 40-34 — **"ECCLESIASTES UNCOVERED!"** (The New MAGNIFIED Version of Ecclesiastes and the Song of Solomon in Plain English!) Book 034. (This is the Book that contains the Famous Sayings for *"There is a Time to be Born, and a Time to Die ..."* which has been Greatly Magnified!)

[_] 40-35 — **"The Environmentalists' Paradise!"** (HOW almost Everyone could be Living in a Beautiful Manmade Paradise!) By The Worldwide People's Revolution!® Book 035. (This Book contains the NMV of *Psalm 48,* which will Amaze you, O Lady Doubtfulness!)

[_] 40-36 — **"The Seven Basic Spiritual Building Blocks of LIFE!"** (Faith Hope Trust Love Patience Persistence and Obedience!) Book 036. (This Book contains the Mockingbird's Version of *Hebrews 11,* plus the NMV of *First Corinthians 13,* among many other "Goodies.")

[_] 40-37 — **"DIETS!"** (A Reasonable Solution for the "Eternal Controversy"!) By The Worldwide People's Revolution!® Book 037.

[_] 40-38 — **"The Nature of CAPITALISM!"** (A List of the EVILS of CAPITALISM!) Book 038.

(A List of the EVILS of CAPITALISM!)

[_] 40-39 — **"SWANGKEENOMIKS Rules the Roost!" (HOW all People can Prosper in a RIIT WAA, and STOP Polluting the Earth with Capitalist TRASH!) By The Worldwide People's Revolution!®** Book 039. (The Cover Photo shows a Portion of our Retirement Home, before the 5,000+ square-feet Concrete Roof was Installed, after moving more than 66 Million Pounds by Hand!)

[_] 40-40 — **"The New MAGNIFIED Version of The Book of MORMON!" (The Story of the White and Dark Indians in the Americas!)** Book 040, which comes in 2 Volumes of about 500 Pages, each. The Cover Photo on the First Volume shows the Queen of England's Golden Coach, and the Cover Photo on the Second Volume shows one of many Polished Spanish Marble Walls in our Selected King's Retirement Home, which is worth a thousand dollars per square yard, which is another Example of what you can also have, if you simply OBEY your Righteous KING! All such Marble is very Inspiring. No one could Study it for very long without Believing in a Great Creator God. The Picture does not do it Justice. You would have to See it in Person, and Wash it with Pure Water to bring Out the Beauty.

[_] 40-41 — **"The GREAT Worldwide TELEVISED Court HEARING!" (That Great Meeting of the Most Intelligent and Wel-Ejukaatid Miindz!) By The Worldwide People's Revolution!®** Book 041. {This is the Book that the World has long been Waiting for: beCause it will Overthrow the Evil Empires, and make it Possible to Establish **"The New RIGHTEOUS One-World Government!" (HOW to Establish a Righteous One-World Government without Going to WAR!) By The Worldwide People's Revolution!®** Book 056. This is the Greatest Idea since the Invention of the Light Bulb, Guaranteed!}

[_] 40-42 — **"The Secret City of the Great King!" (HOW the True Church will Escape from the Great Tribulation!) By The Worldwide People's Revolution!®** Book 042. (Be Sure to Inform your Friends, Relatives and Naaberz about this Wonderful Book: beCause they might also Want to Escape!)

[_] 40-43 — **"Terrorists Beware that your Days are Numbered!" (HOW to Bring those Terrorist Attacks to a Screeching HALT!) By The Worldwide People's Revolution!®** Book 043. (This Book also contains the Fascinating Book of LEHI, which has now been Restored!) †‡

[_] 40-44 — **"The New MAGNIFIED Version of ISAIAH in Plain English!" (The Understandable Version of the Book of Isaiah!)** Book 044. (The Cover Photo shows a Swanky Potato and Avocado Salad with Sweet Peas and Corn, among other "Secret" Ingredients, which are Revealed within the Book. Remember that you can read many Words for Free in the Book Previews on Amazon.com.usa.)

[_] 40-45 — **"HOW to Become a HOLY Man!" (40 Good Reasons WHY People Should FAST and PRAY!)** Book 045, which is a Companion Book of:

[_] 40-46 — **"The Proper RULES for FASTING!" (The Complete Instruction Manual for True Repentance!) By The Worldwide People's Revolution!®** Book 046, which is a Companion Book of the above mentioned Book, which contains a True Life Story about an Old Black Mare called Lucy, who Fasted for 30 Days without Food nor Water, who was Physiologically "Born Again," as Jesus might say. See the Full Details in: **"The New**

87

MAGNIFIED Version of The GOOD NEWS According to Saint JOHN!" (The Gospel According to Saint John Zebedee Boanerges in Plain English!) Book 062, which contains many Inspiring Photographs with Explanations!

[ ] 40-47 — "Are Americans the Most STUPID People who ever Lived?" (HOW Working People can PROSPER and Live in PEACE Under the Rulership of a RIGHTEOUS KING!) By The Worldwide People's Revolution!® Book 047. (The Cover Photo shows a large Portion of the Author's Living Room Floor, which is worth 100,000$, which is just another Good Example of what you can also have, just for Loving and Obeying your Elected King!)

[ ] 40-48 — "An Amazing Collection of Wit and Wisdom!" (The Marvelous Tale of the Colorful Peacock from Angel Ridge, and the Strong Rope of Everlasting Hope!) By The Worldwide People's Revolution!® Book 048. (The Cover Photo shows a Book Display, which will be Greatly Enhanced during the Future, when all 350+ Inspired Books are on Display in a Swanky Truth-brary, as Opposed to the Public LIE-brary.)

[ ] 40-49 — "Justifications for Capitalizations!" (WHY The Worldwide People's Revolution!® Defies the School of Fools by Capitalizing LOVE and HATE!) Book 049.

[ ] 40-50 — "The END of CONFUSION!" (The Great CELEBRATION of the Magnificent Wedding of the Most Humble Honest Nations, and the Grand Year of JUBILEE!) By The Worldwide People's Revolution!® Book 050. (Just Try to Visualize those "Seven Great Swanky Armies of Voluntary Working Soldiers" Marching through the Valley of Megiddo, being Dressed in their Colorful Robes, while the Band Plays *The Battle Hymn of the Republic,* and the Choirs Sing the Praises of the Great KING of Kings! What a Sight and Sound that will be, which will be Climaxed in "The Great World TEMPLE of PEACE," when the Nations will get Married, along with our Elected King! Come one, come all to "The Great Worldwide TELEVISED Court HEARING," by Means of your Wide Flat-screen TVs, whereby you might Learn WHY, WHEN and HOW!) †‡

[ ] 40-51 — "The Loathsome Burdens of the Independent Jackasses!" (A New Civilized Approach for Quietly Solving our Massive Problems!) By The Worldwide People's Revolution!® Book 051. (Just Think about the Multitude of almost Worthless Meetings of the Minds, who Strained themselves to Think of Reasonable Solutions for our Massive Problems, who sometimes even Prayed to God for Help; but, the Solutions have been here for no less than 40 Years — Thanks to the Spirit of Inspiration from GOD!)

[ ] 40-52 — "Are we Tax Slaves of a Lower Order than those Lying Edomites!" (HOW to be Liberated from all Slavery, Worldwide!) By The Worldwide People's Revolution!® Book 052. {This Inspired Book once had another Title and Author, which was not Acceptable by Amazon, which has now been Restored in all of its Glory, and is Published by more Trustworthy People, who are not Afraid of Controversies, nor of: "The Swanky Sword of Divine Truths!" (The Most Powerful Weapon in the Whole Universe!) By The Worldwide People's Revolution!® Book 067.}

[ ] 40-53 — "The Great False Economy is now DEBUNKED!" (Adolf Hitler had a much Better Economic System!) By The Worldwide People's Revolution!® Book 053. (Trust me,

Adolf was no Saint; but, during the Day of God's Judgment, he will be Justified, while his Anti-Christ Opponents will be Condemned: beCause they Refused to Attend a Worldwide Radio Debate with Adolf Hitler, whose Arguments will Stand Up during the Day of Judgment, which would have Prevented World War 2, and thus Saved the Lives of no less than 60 Million People! Likewise, we Tax Slaves must now Act more Wisely, and DEMAND **"The Great Worldwide TELEVISED Court HEARING,"** Book 041, whereby we might Save the World from that Dreadful Battle of Megiddo, called *Armageddon!* Yes, the Ball is now in YOUR Hands, my Potential Friend or Enemy, and you are now Responsible for it. Therefore, do not Shirk your Duty as a Free Citizen; but, Help us to Spread this Message far and wide, whereby the Masses of People will be Demanding The GWTCH, and thus Prevent another far more Dreadful and Hateful World WAR!)

[_] 40-54 — **"The UGLY Scarred Dishonest Face of Poor Old Miserable UNCLE SAM!" (A Memorial Day Legacy!) By The Worldwide People's Revolution!®** Book 054. {NOTE: This Inspired Book was also Suppressed by Amazon, who will be most Ashamed of themselves if they do not Un-suppress it during the Future: beCause it will also be Published by People of Greater Faith, who Know for a Fact that it is the TRUTH! Therefore, just be Patient.}

[_] 40-55 — **"The United States of the Whole World!" (A True Global Economy for the Masses of Working People!) By The Worldwide People's Revolution!®** Book 055. (This Inspired Book contains many Colored Photographs with Explanations. It is a Good Book to Publish in Foreign Nations, who are not so Blinded by their Pride, who can See the Mountain of Lies much Better at a Distance from them: beCause of not being a Part of the American Corruption.) †‡

[_] 40-56 — **"The New RIGHTEOUS One-World Government!" (HOW to Establish a Righteous One-World Government without Going to WAR!) By The Worldwide People's Revolution!®** Book 056. (This is a KEY Book, which everyone should Study Carefully and Prayerfully.)

[_] 40-57 — **"Those Ridiculous Contradictions within the Holy Bible!" (HOW to Read the Mutilated Bible with an Open Mind!) By The Worldwide People's Revolution!®** Book 057. (Many Professing "Christians" Falsely Claim that their so-called *"Holy Bibles"* do not Contain any Contradictions, being "the Infallible Inspired Word of the Living God," but, without the Capitalized Words, and without Explaining just WHY there are more than 200 Contradictory Versions of it! This Book Reveals how to Deal with those Biblical Problems, and come to Understand WHY God Allowed it to Happen for the Truth's Sake. Trust me, you have never Heard this Explanation before now.)

[_] 40-58 — **"The Divided States of United Lies!" (The so-called "United States of North America" in Disguise!) By The Worldwide People's Revolution!®** Book 058. {NOTE: This is perhaps the most Referred to Book among all of the Books by our Selected King; but, that does not Mean that it is his Best Book by any Means, which is Well Camouflaged: so that it will Survive the Test of Time, even if the others are BURNED by the Anti-Christ Followers of Satan, who are Possession Worshipers of the Worst Kind, who Seek to Justify American Lies, rather than Quickly Confess them, and thus Escape from their Self-made Prison of Propagandish Lies! Just be Perfectly Honest, and you will have no Problem with any of our Literature.}

[_] 40-59 — "**The Complete SURVEYS of our VALUES!**" (SURVEYS of Religious Spiritual Political Governmental Sexual Social Moral Economic Business Labor Habitual and Miscellaneous VALUES!) By The Worldwide People's Revolution!® Book 059. {NOTE: According to our Selected King, every Potential Leader in the World must Fill Out and File those Surveys on the Internet for everyone to Study, whereby the Best People might be Elected by those Wise People who have also Filled Out the Complete Surveys of their own Values, whereby they will be Qualified to VOTE. Otherwise, they will not be Qualified to Vote, which will Eliminate a LOT of Wasted Money on Election Deceptions, while at the same Time it will Educate a lot of Ignorant People, who Desperately Need to Study that Inspired Book before Voting for another Dimwitcrat, Reprobate, or Independent Jackass!}

[_] 40-60 — "**HOW to Get our PRIORITIES in ORDER!**" (The Glories of Democracy; and, Does DEMON-ocracy have its Priorities in Order?) By The Worldwide People's Revolution!® Book 060. This Book will need to be Re-written by a Collective Group of Wise People, who will Contribute their True Life Stories during the Future, when they Wake Up and come to their Right Senses with the Prodigal Son of *Luke 15*. See:

[_] 40-61 — "**The New MAGIFIED Version of The GOOD NEWS According to Saint LUKE!**" (The Magnified Gospel of Saint Luke in Plain English!) Book 061, which is by Far the Best Version of that Gospel on the Earth, which has no Rivals at all among the other 200+ Versions. Guaranteed!

[_] 40-62 — "**The New MAGNIFIED Version of The GOOD NEWS According to Saint JOHN!**" (The Gospel According to Saint John Zebedee Boanerges in Plain English!) Book 062, which also has no Rivals among all of the other Versions: beCause this is no Translation of anything; but, it is the Inspired Words of the Living God, which were Revealed by the Holy Spirit, who has not Died.

[_] 40-63 — "**The New MAGNIFIED Version of the Book of ACTS!**" (The Understandable Version of the Acts of the Apostles in Plain English!) By The Worldwide People's Revolution!® Book 063. (This Inspired Book makes it Understandable WHY the Jews Hated the Apostles so much. You will have to Read it to Believe it.)

[_] 40-64 — "**The New MAGNIFIED Version of the PSALMS of King David!**" (The Understandable Version of the Famous Psalms in Plain English!) Book 064. You will be Amazed!

[_] 40-65 — "**A List of FAIR Swanky Wages!**" (The Equitable Wage System!) By The Worldwide People's Revolution!® Book 065. (All Hardworking People will LOVE this Good Book!)

[_] 40-66 — "**Beautiful Swanky PALACES!**" (A New Concept in Living Habits — Swanky Palaces for Poor People!) By The Worldwide People's Revolution!® Book 066. (You have no Idea what a "Swanky Palace" IS, unless you have read this Unique Book.)

[_] 40-67 — "**The Swanky Sword of Divine Truths!**" (The Most Powerful Weapon in the Whole Universe!) Book 067. (The very Reason that our Selected King has no Rivals is beCause

(A List of the EVILS of CAPITALISM!)

of the Swanky Sword of Divine Truths, which no one can Defeat by any Means. Therefore, you Need to have it on your own Side, whereby no one can Defeat your Arguments! Be Strong, be Brave, have Faith and put on the Whole Armor of GOD!)

[_] 40-68 — **"Has your Life become Extremely Complicated?" (HOW to Live a SIMPLE Life!) By The Worldwide People's Revolution!®** Book 068. (Many People are not even Aware of just how Complicated their Lives are, until suddenly they are ready to Commit Suicide! It is Best to Prevent all such Evil Things, and this Book tells HOW.)

[_] 40-69 — **"The IDEAL Place to Live!" (HOW to Discover the Ideal Place to Live!)** Book 069.

[_] 40-70 — **"Our Elected King Who Speaks Out!" (It is High Time for some Sane Person to Get Control of this Insane World!) By The Worldwide People's Revolution!®** Book 070. (This Inspired Book contains a Special Speech that is Addressed to both Houses of the Congress in Washington. You will Love it, O Man of Greater Faith!)

[_] 40-71 — **"How GAY is GOD?" (Oh the Wonders of it all when it ALL Hangs Out!)** Book 071. (Do not Judge the Book, until you have Carefully "Red" all of it. You will be Surprised by the Truths!)

[_] 40-72 — **"LIGHTNING STRIKES Versus Lightning Bugs and Impotent Fireflies!" (A Memorial Photo Album of some Real American Heroes!) By The Worldwide People's Revolution!®** Book 072. (NOTE: This Book is Unique among all of the Books by our Selected King: beCause he did not get to Proof-read it before the Computer Crashed. It just Happened to be Saved on a Computer Chip before the Computer Crashed, and therefore it was Saved in PDF. But, the Corrections did not get made, which makes it a Special Collector's Item, which has more than 100 Colored Photos, which was what Caused the Crash.) †‡

[_] 40-73 — **"The BEST of CAPITALISM!" (Corrections for: "LIGHTNING STRIKES Versus Lightning Bugs and Impotent Fireflies!")** Book 073. (It is a completely new Book, except for those Corrections; and it is one of the Best Books in the World, which all Honest People will Love.)

[_] 40-74 — **"LIGHTNING STRIKES Versus Lightning Bugs!" (HOW you can Become Moderately RICH, without Telling any Lies nor Selling any Trash!) By The Worldwide People's Revolution!®** Book 074, which is the Perfection of all of the Lightning Striking Books, which is Recommended above all others for Mass Production: beCause it stands the Best Chance of being a Real Winner, just after this Book that you are now Reading, which has a Magnetizing Title!

[_] 40-75 — **"What are the Punishments for Dietary Sins?" (Have we Served ourselves Well at the Tables of our Lusts?)** Book 075. (This Book is too Controversial to be Published at this Time. Be very Patient until it is Available: beCause it is HOT!)

[_] 40-76 — **"What is WRong with those CRAZY CHRISTIANS?" (A Self-Examination of the Heart of the Body of Good Government!) By The Worldwide People's Revolution!®** Book 076.

[ ] 40-77 — **"The Gospel According to our Elected King!" (The Good News from the Most Modern Perspective!)** Book 077. (This is perhaps the Best Book that you will Discover on Amazon, which contains the Famous Sermon that Jonah gave to the Ninevites, plus a very Special Sermon by Jesus Christ, himself!)

[ ] 40-78 — **"The Root Cause for almost all Evils!" (The Strange Things that People Say and Do to Get more Money!)** Book 078. (This Book contains many Colored Photographs with Fascinating Explanations!)

[ ] 40-79 — **"Orgimmick Gardening at its Best!" (HOW to Grow Delicious Satisfying Foods without a 10-Million-Dollar Investment!) By The Worldwide People's Revolution!®** Book 079. (This Book also contains many Colored Photographs with Wonderful Explanations!)

[ ] 40-80 — **"Guaranteed Solutions!" (HOW to Solve our Local and Global Problems in the Most Rational Manner Possible!)** Book 080. (See the Description on Amazon: because they Offer a ONE-MILLION-DOLLAR REWARD to anyone who can Prove our Selected King's Solutions to be WRong or Unworkable! Can you Beat that? Do you have all such Guaranteed Solutions? Only our Selected King has those Solutions: beCause God Blest him with those Provable Solutions, which can be Proven in any Courtroom with Law and Order.)

[ ] 40-81 — **"Mexicans are more Intelligent than Americans!" (A Unique Challenge to all Americans and Mexicans!) By The Worldwide People's Revolution!®** Book 081. {NOTE: The Remaining 275 Inspired Books by the Author of this Book may only be found in English, until we can get them Properly Translated into other Languages. Shame on you People who Killed him, who Broke his Heart with your Unbelief. May God have Mercy on your Poor Wretched Souls.} †‡

[ ] 40-82 — **"¡Los Mexicanos son más Inteligentes que los Estadounidenses!" (¡Un Desafío Único para todos los Estadounidenses y Mexicanos!) By The Worldwide People's Revolution!®** Book 082. {NOTA: Aquí está el primer Libro en Español, que puede no ser Perfecto; pero, es Perfectamente lo Suficientemente Bueno para Iluminar las Mentes de quien lo Estudia.}

[ ] 40-83 — **"Was Billy Graham Greatly Deceived?" (Giving Honor to whom Honor is Due!) By The Worldwide People's Revolution!®** Book 083. {NOTE: If you know a Grahamite, please Direct him or her to this Inspired Book, whereby he or she might be Converted to the Truths within it, and thus be Saved from Grahamite Perversions. Thank you.}

[ ] 40-84 — **"The New MAGNIFIED Version of the Book of DEUTERONOMY!" (The Understandable Version of Deuteronomy in Plain English!)** Book 084. This is actually one of the Best Books within the entire Holy Bible, and also one of the Longest; but, do not allow that Fact to Deter you by any Means: beCause, "the Bigger Book is Normally a Better Book," which is True of a lot of Books, including all of the above Books: beCause it is the Nature of the Holy Spirit to get into Long-winded Sermons, you might say, which is WHY the Apostle Paul Preached until Midnight in the Book of Acts, until some Boy fell from a Window and Killed himself, whom the Apostle Paul Raised Up from the Dead and went on Preaching until the Dawn of the Day!

(A List of the EVILS of CAPITALISM!)

{See: **"The New MAGNIFIED Version of the Book of ACTS"** for the Finest of Details, Book 063.}

[_] 40-85 — **"All of the Arguments are in Favor of our Selected King, who has Zero Challengers!" (Before you Attend another Election Deception, you should Carefully Study this Inspired Book with an Honest Open Mind!) By The Worldwide People's Revolution!®** Book 085.

[_] 40-90 — **"A New Jerusalem in the Great State of Flexible Texas!" (HOW to make Good Use of the Mississippi River!) By The Worldwide People's Revolution!** Book 090.

Your Personal List of the Evils of Capitalism

(A List of the EVILS of CAPITALISM!)

The Enticement,

Our Selected King, has Listed some of the Chief Evils of Capitalism within this Inspired Book; but, the List could go on and on and ON: beCause the Capitalists are Continually Inventing New Evils, and Greater and Greater Injustices, Worldwide. Indeed, it is the Nature of Capitalism to make Things Worse and WORSE, rather than Produce Healthy Happy People, who are Free from Education Slavery, Work Slavery, Tax Slavery, Interest Slavery, Insurance Slavery, Drug Slavery, Food Bills Slavery, Water Bills Slavery, Gas Bills Slavery, ElecTrickery Bills Slavery, Entertainment Bills Slavery, Repair Bills Slavery, and all other Kinds of SLAVERY. Indeed, Slavery is / was / and will always be the Chief Sin of Capitalism: beCause it cannot Resist the Great Temptation to take Advantage of other People, and Especially of IGNORANT People, who Imagine that they are Educated with a Capital E, and Free with a Capital F, when they are nothing but SLAVES of an EVIL Capitalist EMPIRE, who can now be Liberated with a Capital L, and Set Free with a Capital F, as Jesus Christ would say! The Great Question is, "Do you Believe it?" If so, please do your Best to Inform other Slaves about it.